THE
GOD
PLACE

Finding Peace & Enjoying Life In A Stressful World

BOB GASSMAN

Disclaimer: Neither the publisher nor the author are engaged in rendering professional advice or
services through this book. The ideas, recommendations, and suggestions are not intended to be a
substitution for consulting with a professional health care practitioner. The publisher and author
shall not be liable or responsible for any loss or damage allegedly arising from the information or
suggestions in this book.

CONTENTS

FOREWORD

An ancient Chinese proverb says, "When a wise man points to the moon, the idiot looks at the finger." Professor John Lawrence Hill observes we have become expert idiots. We live in an age when our knowledge of how things are in physical reality has reached levels inconceivable a few decades ago, while our knowledge of the why of reality has nearly faded from view. Bob Gassman has pointed a finger at the moon. I invite you to join the wise ones who will not focus on the finger but seek the luminescence he wants us to see.

We love to debate what is "real." Our current philosophies and worldviews justify this debate because the prevailing wisdom is that there is no objective, transcendent reality. We construct it socially and religiously: it varies based on social and religious viewpoints. This is fair game, (goes the contemporary argument) because there is no single, unassailable reality that one can claim or experience. But run your car into a wall and you will discover reality is more than socially constructed! By its nature and definition, it sits out there regardless of whether or not you believe it, want it, or perceive it. Life will go better if we accept it, believe it, and then learn how to interact with what is truly real.

Bob has written a book about reality. He has used the societal epidemic of stress as a pathway that leads to and invites us into a relationship with what is ultimately real. Indeed, as Bob clearly demonstrates, much of our stress and all of its strength lies in our fading knowledge of the nature of the universe and world in which we live, move, and have our being.

Although philosophies and religions all have a creation story, the beginning of our universe is a highly developed and well-characterized body of scientific knowledge. The Big Bang Theory has become accepted science based on the sheer breadth and depth of cosmological evidence. This is not to say it is welcomed by much of the scientific and philosophical communities, but reality, as I say, does not need our approbation, affection, or even our belief to be real. That a creation event took place billions of years ago is evident in the data. It follows that there must be a creator, a "first cause" as Socrates and Plato called it. Most often, this creator is simply called God.

This is not a religious issue. Religion is what follows when humans endeavor to describe the nature of the Creator's purposes, expectations, and plans in its dealing with the world and humankind. The existence of a creator is simply unassailable in the presence of a creation. Bob Gassman offers to us living in the 21st century an ancient answer to our contemporary epidemic of stress: it is simply to cry out to the Creator for help. If this lacks the feeling of something innovative and new, that's because it is not new. Humans have been crying out to God for thousands of years. As the saying goes, there are no atheists in foxholes. And we have been digging foxholes since we first encountered threats to happiness beyond our own capacity to battle and overcome. The presence of trouble is common to humankind. No one is immune. Everyone will be afflicted. After years of sociological, psychological, pharmacological, religious, philosophical, and new age stress-relief offerings, we find ourselves in ever-increasing levels of stress as individuals and societies. Perhaps it is time we try something different. Not new, but decidedly different in our time.

Steven E. Carter, Ph.D. July 2019

INTRODUCTION

This book is part of the revival of an ancient but powerful truth. New light is shining on something tangible, something real. It is both radical and revolutionary. The intent of the book is not to kindle a new movement; the movement is already happening. It is similar to a train slowly pulling away from the station where the conductor with an outstretched hand is hollering, "All aboard!" I encourage you to jump on board and take a ride: to explore something you have perhaps never considered. If you don't think this book will make an impact on your life, well, you can always keep doing what you are doing.

AN INVITATION TO THE "WHOEVER"

We are all seekers whether we admit it or not. We are hardwired that way. This book evolved from seeking solutions for the ever-rising epidemic of stress, and from discovering the secret to absolute deliverance from it. My friends and colleagues wanted to know if the book was addressed to any specific genre. It is neither tailored nor targeted to any particular group of people, but it is an open invitation to anyone—the "whoever." (I will define the idea of "whoever" in Chapter One.) This is a pretty wide audience, I know. But all are welcome to explore! No matter who you are, you will benefit from this book's insights as your eyes are opened and your understanding is enriched.

In this book, *The God Place*, we are going to examine how to overcome stress through an approach not talked about in common self-help writings or scientific literature. The simplicity of this approach is only exceeded by its effectiveness. We are going to journey down an ancient but opportune path from stress to freedom. This path leads to reality and will introduce us to the heart of the one who created us and the universe in which we really live. We will enter into a real relationship with this creator. While there are many names used to describe this creator of all things, this book uses the expression God. This is not a self-help book but a God-help book. We are going to find out what God is truly like. We will discover his real nature and character.

There are many ways God declares himself. If we emphasize one of these ways over another, or are insensitive to his diversity of communication and expression, then we will limit all he has for us. Having said this, I confess that the book heavily references the Scriptures: the Old and New Testament. They are among God's precious gifts to the "whoever." These truths were not reserved for some esoteric group of people. Yet long before the Scriptures were written, God was already revealing his heart to humanity. Over the centuries, people from every culture have discovered and practiced many of these truths and passed them down to subsequent generations. God is real; He makes himself known to the seeker. He will demonstrate his love, joy, peace, goodness, comfort, guidance, and so much more. Are you curious to find out how a relationship with this creator applies to your stress?

God does not overstep our freedom of will. This is a very important truth to acknowledge. Our power to choose is another one of God's gifts to every human being. Despite our response, he lovingly and unconditionally pursues everyone, the "whoevers," you and me, and invites us into the reality of his presence. This is the foundation of what I call the *God Place*. When I first began to define the *God Place*, I was visiting an esteemed friend, Dr. Sammy Linge in Nairobi, Kenya. He has been a college professor, chancellor and great community leader. But above those accolades, he is a brilliant thinker. A discussion ensued about why people put God in a box. I mentioned to him that I wanted to think outside the box regarding the theme of the *God Place*. In reply, Dr. Sammy articulated, "What is this box? Why don't we just get rid of the box altogether and think freely?" Dr. Sammy is right: let's get rid of any box we have put God in and think freely!

Human beings default to places of safety: we seek protection from suffering, hurt, pain and harm. When the word "God" is brought up in conversation it immediately elicits all kinds of thoughts, memories and imagery. For many people, certain religious experiences have caused hurt—and unfortunately the blame has been put on God. There are those who want nothing to do with God because they associate him with pain. Since we don't want to be hurt, we avoid the source of what we perceive to cause the pain. Most people carry their negative religious experiences around in "buckets" containing stagnant waters of traditions, preconceived ideas and misconceptions. But we can empty those buckets and let God fill them to overflowing with his pure, fresh and living water.

The God Place is a deliberate positioning and designation of our hearts and minds.

The *God Place* is not confined to or defined by a physical location, although it certainly may include one. It could be a peaceful setting in nature or personal headspace, even in the midst of a crowded airport terminal. The *God Place* is a deliberate positioning and designation of our hearts and minds. The *God Place* is a state of being where a true and personal connection takes place with the Creator of the universe! God is always ready to receive us at any given moment. He welcomes us with open arms just as we are and where we are. Here's the truth: God is simple; religion makes God complicated. God is after relationship, not religion!

God doesn't shun, discriminate or show partiality to the seeker. That's why the *God Place* is a haven of help, a sanctuary of safety and a resort of refuge where we can "pour out our hearts." God will take us as far as we desire and escort us into an open, roomy space of freedom. Whether we are mildly stressed or falling apart at the seams, the *God*

Place is for you and me: the "whoevers."

Maybe you are stuck in the relentless routine of rituals or tired of useless traditions defined and regulated by other people. Perhaps you want to cultivate a deeper relationship with your Creator, who

God is after relationship, not religion. wants to help deliver you from stress. Whatever your situation, this book will encourage you to seek, ponder, explore and experience solutions from God.

Do you have an appetite for more—much, much more? Then turn the page, and get ready for an upgrade in your journey. You will be transformed by finding peace and enjoying life in a stressful world. Welcome to the *God Place*.

CHAPTER 1

DEFINITION OF STRESS

Years ago I had a nutrition practice in a small Connecticut town. Doctors referred patients to me for nutritional therapy. As I initially interviewed the patients, I began to realize that around ninety percent of them acknowledged they experienced stress. They believed it was affecting their health and well-being.

It's not surprising that people suffer from stress. Professional publications, including the *Journal of the American Medical Association* and *Psychology Today,* report that seventy-five to ninety percent of all doctor's office visits are for stress-related ailments and complaints. Current research suggests that stress wreaks havoc on every organ in our bodies, including (and perhaps most importantly) our brains. Its effect even reaches deep into the cellular level and slows down the rate of healing our bodies and minds. Stress also inhibits our ability to maintain good health. OSHA, the Occupational Safety and Health Administration, includes stress as a hazard in the workplace. According to the World Health Organization, stress costs American industry more than $300 billion annually due to sickness.

In order to help my patients, I developed individualized plans for lifestyle changes and implemented dietary and nutritional protocols. Frequently the methods worked and people got somewhat better, but there was still something missing. Even though their symptoms improved, the cause of their stress was not addressed. Could there be a better solution, something more, something exceptional?

A NEW REVELATION

One morning, I was in my office contemplating this matter. Pondering deeper thoughts had become a regular activity for me, and this particular day was graciously suited for seeking solutions to stress. My office was designed to be a quiet haven for both my patients and me, offering an inviting atmosphere of freedom to unleash concerns about practically anything. I delighted in the prospect of finding answers as I peered out the two windows overlooking the woods. The windows were cracked open, and a fresh, cool breeze stroked my cheeks as I took in the natural beauty of the outdoors. As the sun softly glistened off the autumn leaves, it was as though time stood still. The peaceful moment brought an awareness of God's presence, and I felt as though he was about to speak. I call this delightful experience the *God Place*. As mentioned in the introduction, the *God Place* is a deliberate positioning and designation of the heart and mind. It is a state of being where a true and personal connection takes place with the Creator of the universe!

God gently embraced my heart, yet in a confrontational tone inquired, "Aren't you interested in what I have to say about stress?"

Suddenly, the very wind of heaven arose in the breeze. The leaves scurried across the ground and vied for my attention. God gently embraced my heart, yet in a confrontational tone inquired, "Aren't you interested in what I have to say about stress?"

The desire to get God's perspective was like the morning sun, slowly rising above the horizon. More and more light appeared, entering my mind and illuminating my heart with wisdom from above. My spirit leaped within me and on that day I embarked on a mission, a journey of seeking to discover God's heart and perspective regarding this very urgent topic. I recalled that God's thoughts and ways are far higher than any human being's wisdom and began the quest of seeking him for answers. This involved conversations with God, word studies comparing biblical translations, secular literature and discussions with others. I deliberately chose to search the Scriptures (the Bible) as part of my quest because they reflect the heart of God, including his thoughts, logic and understanding. Additionally, the Scriptures have been revered and regarded as authoritative by people around the world for thousands of years. The wisdom found within the Scriptures have withstood the test of time. The discovery of a truth revealed a reoccurring theme. My findings are supported by biblical stories of real people.

I soon discovered that God was so gracious, good and kind that when a "whoever" (like you and me), called out to him, he responded with help. God's invitation is to the "whoever." He neither limits this invitation to a select group of people, nor makes anyone jump through hoops to find him. There are, however, certain conditions that must be accepted by the "whoever." They are not burdensome, but they are necessary to enter the *God Place*. Here's a simple example. Whoever comes to God must believe that he is real and that it is a worthwhile investment to seek him. Why? Because he cares enough about each seeker to respond with his personal and generous benevolence. We are all seeking something aren't we? If you don't believe these truths or are unwilling to explore these realities, then, at this moment, you might not find this book very useful. Let me share a little story about a "seeker" with you.

One Sunday morning I was walking our dog around the block. A neighbor came out of her house with her dog and walked along with me. She said she had to hurry because she needed to get ready for church. As we walked, she asked, "So what are you doing today?" I told her that I was sitting with God and asking him for direction on some matters, and then planning on reading a book about the soul.

She said, "My soul is not at peace."

I waited.

"My husband and I are facing some decisions. We think maybe a change in geography might relieve some of the stress."

"Do you think changing locations will change what is going on in your heart?" I asked. God prompted me to say a bit more: "Perhaps God is using this situation to invite you into a deeper relationship. Maybe that includes moving, or maybe not: if you go to God about these decisions he will provide clear direction and make your path smooth."

"How do you go to God?" she asked.

"Well, you could simply sit with him. It's a relationship, not a formula. You can allow God's peace to rule over your heart—and peace is a gauge and an indicator of making right decisions."

She replied, "These words are making my soul feel 100 pounds lighter!" (And she is a petite woman!) Then she stopped in her tracks. "Do you mean I don't need to go to church to meet with God?"

I responded that God is present and available 24/7, anytime and anywhere. He is not restricted to a location or time. She confided that she felt guilty skipping church and was worried that God would not be pleased.

My neighbor is like millions of "whoevers" around the world. They are seekers on a journey to find the *God Place*.

Our quest of seeking God provides rich dividends that can prove to be an everyday experience. These benefits include discovering the path that leads to the unfolding revelation of God's solution to stress.

I decided to offer this revelation to patients in addition to the normal nutritional protocols. Out of respect for others' religious preferences, I asked whether they wanted to include God's perspective as part of their individualized plan. Most agreed, and as my patients carried out these recommendations, they realized great deliverance from stress. As they addressed both their symptoms and the underlying cause of those symptoms they discovered their path to freedom.

It was an awesome experience to witness these exhilarating results. For example, there was a woman, whom I will call Rebecca. She was a dedicated homemaker in her mid-thirties and a police officer who worked in the local community. Over the course of her career she developed work-related stress which was compounded by a broken marriage. Because of escalating emotional issues, she was relieved from active duty and put behind a desk. She had been experiencing problems associated with being overweight and also dealing with the enormous stress of being a first responder. I suggested she incorporate a protocol to seek godly wisdom, and she agreed to give it a try, even though she had not considered this as a possible solution to her stress. As we began our work together, she confided that she had not spoken with her sister in twenty years because of a dispute over an inheritance. She said the lack of communication with her sibling was eating away at her, and this distraught feeling exacerbated the stress she experienced on the job.

As these overbearing feelings occupied her mind, she sought relief through overeating. Like many people, she self-medicated her stress by eating refined carbohydrates (mostly products made with white sugar and/or white flour) to light up the pleasure centers of the brain and provide temporary relief. But what goes up must come down, and as the good feeling wore off, the stress returned—and with it the craving for more refined carbohydrates. Indulgence in these kinds of foods elicits an insulin response which stores fat and triggers a hunger signal to eat more. This vicious cycle leads to everything from weight gain to mood swings.

I discussed a scriptural reference with her which says, "Never worry about anything. But in every situation let God know what you need in prayers and requests while giving thanks. Then God's peace, which goes beyond anything we can imagine, will guard your thoughts and emotions through Christ Jesus."[1]

She responded with delight, so I continued to encourage her, saying, "Go to God with your problems. Ask him what to do." (My inspiration for this advice came from the book of James. "But if any of you lack wisdom, you should pray to God, who will give it to you; because God gives generously and graciously to all. But when you pray, you must believe and not doubt at all. Whoever doubts is like a wave in the sea that is driven and blown about by the wind. If you are like that, unable to make up your mind and undecided in all you do, you must not think that you will receive anything from the Lord."[2])

I watched her countenance change as new understanding flooded her soul. She exclaimed that she was going to apply these recommendations to what she felt was God's direction for her life. That very afternoon she called her sister. They had a conversation for the first time in decades. As they spoke, apologies were exchanged, bitterness was unraveled, forgiveness emerged, and the beginning of reconciliation blossomed. This conversation relieved an undeterminable amount of stress from her life and gave her a new outlook and hope. Additionally, she decided to stop remedying her stress through the short-lived solution of overeating. As a result, she experienced wholeness as she reconnected to God, and benefited from weight loss and other improvements in her physical and emotional well-being.

As Rebecca was rescued from stress, she found strength to follow through on sensible health choices. It changed her life. But why do we need to be rescued from stress? Why not just cope with it and accept that it is a part of life?

STRESS IS PERVASIVE

Stress affects everyone: young and old, rich and poor, male and female, every race, every nationality and every culture. It is an equal opportunity destroyer; nobody is immune. Life can be overwhelming. Daily conflicts can develop into mental, emotional, spiritual and physical storms. The instability of our world adds more pressure. We are overworked, in debt and exhausted. It is no wonder so many are drawn toward temporary solutions that promise immediate relief: drugs, alcohol, food, sexual indulgence, television and the Internet.

We are seeking solutions. We are crying out for help. We need a light to lead us from our troubles to peace. The world offers its opinions and wisdom in the area of stress reduction; just as I offered solutions with nutritional remedies. There are many treatments for relieving stress. Recommendations include medications, exercise programs, bio-feedback techniques and psychosocial therapies—everything from yogurt to yoga. But stress is not just rooted in psychological or physiological problems. It also involves spiritual matters, which suggests why God's solutions can be, quite literally, life-saving. There is a better solution. You do not need to be a victim to stress. This book charts your roadmap to victory!

We need a light to lead us from our troubles to peace.

At the same time, this book is not meant to rival or trivialize other solutions. Rather, the focus is on understanding how to overcome stress through God's solutions. It doesn't matter who you are, your age, your religious beliefs, where you have been or what you have done. All that matters is this: where do you want to go from here?

This is your invitation to begin a spiritual journey toward alleviating stress in your life. The keys in this book will help you apply God's solutions, and these solutions will result in relief from stress in many ways.

Are you ready to begin this journey? You will need to confront the reality of stress in your life and what might be causing it. You will learn how to find the *God Place* and how to go to it. The *God Place* will bring about positive outcomes in your life. You are about to move in the right direction toward successfully overcoming stress.

DEFINING STRESS

My family and I lived in a beautiful four-bedroom home on two acres, and both the house and the land required regular maintenance. The New England winter had been unusually harsh one year but was finally loosening its grip after a long, snowy season. The time had come to take down the storm windows and put up the screens again. Spring was in the air and it felt invigorating. The balmy southwest winds and budding leaves confirmed that the warm season was upon us, arousing within me a sudden passion to take care of a long list of chores. Eager to get underway, I drove to the local shopping center to buy certain items at the country hardware store.

After getting the supplies I needed, I casually walked back outside into the warm, sunny day. Suddenly, I was nearly bowled over by a teenage girl bolting past me while ranting into her cell phone, "I am so stressed out! It's been ten whole minutes since my boyfriend has called me!" She was frantic and utterly oblivious to how close she'd come to colliding with me.

It doesn't matter who you are, your age, your religious beliefs, where you have been or what you have done. All that matters is this: where do you want to go from here?

I shook my head and thought how ridiculous it was for anyone to be that upset over such a little thing. Then I remembered the days of my youth. It may have been pacing by the phone waiting for my girlfriend to call or frantically cramming for an upcoming test at school. What are now trivial matters seemed so traumatic back then. What appears to be the end of the world for one person may be a simple shrug of the shoulder to another. The devastating situation of this non-attentive young lady outside the hardware store was just as stressful for her as an unexpected doctor's report could be for an older adult.

What exactly is stress, and how can we use God's solutions to overcome the stress in our lives?

Let's define our terms.

Stress is a response to an event, condition, experience, or other stimulus. These stressors may be mental, physical, or spiritual and arise from both internal and external circumstances. Examples in today's world include: financial concerns, the demands of longer work-related hours combined with increasing expectations, challenges of family relationships and the crippling fear of what the future holds. God's solutions are answers of how to overcome problems and situations according to his resources and guidance.

Since the word "stress" rarely appears in most translations of the Bible, how can we be assured there are godly solutions for it? The answer lies with the etymology of the word. According to the *Online Etymology Dictionary,* the word "stress" evolved around the 1300's and is, in part, a shortening of the Middle English word "distress." Therefore, the word stress is a derivative of distress, a word frequently used in the Scriptures. We can rely on this biblical foundation as we explore the important topic of overcoming stress through God's solutions.

After examining most verses involving the word "distress," I'd like to propose this biblical rendering: a narrowing, a restriction, trouble, pressure, affliction, oppressed, pressed and confined. It is even used to describe a woman in labor. The reason I offer a biblical rendering of distress is because while words and their meanings are fascinating, they may change over time. It is important to understand that words in the Scriptures may have had different meanings when

9

originally written than the way they are commonly used today. The twenty-second chapter of the book of Numbers adds light to our understanding of stress. "Then the angel of the LORD stood in a path among the vineyards, where there was a wall on either side. And when the donkey saw the angel of the LORD, she pressed herself into the wall, and crushed Balaam's foot against the wall. So he beat her again. Then the angel of the LORD went farther, and stood in a narrow place, where there was no way to turn either to the right or to the left."[3] The word "narrow" in this passage is translated from the Hebrew word *tsar*, which is translated "distress" elsewhere in the Scriptures. Today, we might say, "in dire straits" or "between a rock and a hard place." Certainly, anyone who has experienced stress can relate to this feeling!

Here's one way to understand the word "stress." In the New Life Version, Psalm 31:9a says, "Show me loving-kindness, O Lord, for I am in trouble," while the English Standard Version states, "Be gracious to me, O LORD, for I am in distress." In both translations the Hebrew verb, *tsarar*, is the same primitive root for "trouble" and "distress." In other words, stress can also mean trouble. In Chapter 3, we will look further at verses pertaining to distress and trouble, along with other related words, in order to develop our understanding of what God says about stress and to learn his solutions.

There was a time when I experienced how trouble and stress were intertwined. While completing my internship at Yale-New Haven Hospital, my life was compounded with running a small company, raising a family, and overseeing home church fellowships. One day, I ordered some chemical products for my business. When they arrived at the trucking terminal, I retrieved them with my pickup truck after finishing the day at the hospital.

Being in a rush, I had the warehouse personnel load a pallet of the chemicals onto the back of my truck, but I neglected to check if the pails were properly secured on the pallet. During the drive home, the shrink wrap around the pallet suddenly gave way. I gaped into my rearview mirror with terror as several pails toppled out of the truck bed and onto the highway. Cars swerved left and right to avoid the rolling obstacles.

I quickly pulled to the side of the road. Queasiness overcame my entire body as merciless drivers honked their horns and screamed obscenities at me. I tried to recover the lost pails, but the rush hour traffic was just too intense. Then the "what ifs" began to torment my mind. *What if an accident happens as a result of my carelessness? What if there is a chemical spill?* My company name was on the labeled pails. *Now you're really in big trouble!* I was stressed to the point of hopelessness. The only thing I knew to do was to give the whole disastrous event over to God.

Slipping back into the truck, I exited the highway and took the back roads with a strategy to avoid detection. When I finally got home, I watched the evening news and was relieved to learn that no accidents were reported in relation to the incident. "Whew!" I joyfully exclaimed. "Thank you, God!" Still, I didn't sleep very well that night.

The following day I received a call from the Department of Environmental Protection. Someone had reported the incident, and although the pails were recovered, some of them had spilled. The agency imposed a fine and a fee for the cleanup service as well. When I explained to them what happened, they warned me to be more careful, but sympathetically waived the fine. As I hung up the phone, I realized that the trouble had been lifted and my stress relieved. Sure, things could have been better, but they also could have been a lot worse! And such is life for all of us.

The Bible gives us insights into understanding stress and keeping life in its proper perspective. But stress was certainly around way before the plea in Psalm 31 or the incident recorded in Numbers 22.

When did stress first appear to humanity? Were we designed to be continually under stress? Let's venture back in history and discover the answers.

References

Content taken from: Isaiah 55:9-11; Hebrews 11:6; Proverbs 3:6; and Colossians 3:15

1. Philippians 4:6-7 (GW)

2. James 1:5-8 (GNT)

3. Numbers 22:24-26 (NET)

CHAPTER 2

THE ORIGIN OF STRESS

Is this what the garden of Eden was like? I couldn't help but wonder as I sat outside my hotel in Bujumbura (the capital of Burundi, Africa).

I had awakened before the sun came up. The clean morning air stimulated my senses even more than the freshly brewed cup of Burundian coffee in my hand. A mild, balmy breeze swayed across the palm trees adjacent to a huge lake. As the sun peered over the mountains, its first rays sparkled upon the gentle waves lapping rhythmically against the shore. Birds sang gloriously while other flocks flew in formation silhouetted against the peaceful dawn-lit sky. The land was waking up. It teemed with the sights and sounds of life.

In that tranquil moment, I experienced absolutely no stress (except for perhaps a little caffeine on the adrenal glands). Then I reflected, *Was there stress in the garden of Eden?* I set down my cup and opened my Bible to the Book of Genesis. Reading through the first chapter, I noticed the word "good" was written six times, concluding, "Then God looked over all he had made, and he saw that it was very good!"[1]

"Very good" was God's assessment of all his creation, including Adam and Eve. It is one thing for us to evaluate something and say it is good, but for God to appraise his own handiwork as being "very good" endorses his value of creation. The word "good" carries with it an essence of being bountiful, rich, and prosperous along with the qualities of being happy, at ease, and having favor. Add the adverb "very" to the mix and you incorporate the descriptors of abundantly, exceedingly and mightily to the highest degree.

Wow, God! I thought. *Are you saying that this is what the garden of Eden was like?* Even the word "Eden" is defined as *delight, pleasure and paradise.* This initially describes the *God Place*, a place where the Lord could impart his love and goodness to Adam. Yet Genesis states, "And the Lord God said, 'It isn't good for man to be alone; I will make a companion for him, a helper suited to his needs.'"[2] While Adam had sweet fellowship with his Creator, this vertical (human to God) relationship in the *God Place* was designed to be further enhanced by sharing God through a horizontal (human to human) relationship with Eve. Even today this design holds true. As we seek the *God Place* first, the benefits and blessings of God will overflow into the lives of those around us. The sharing of this godly relationship, both vertically and horizontally, is called "fellowship." One mistake people make is to seek God primarily through others, yet that kind of fellowship is complimentary and can never replace the primary relationship of communing with God.

Genesis also declares that God created man and woman in his image. Adam was a three-part being composed of body, soul, and spirit. The Gospel of John defines God as Spirit. By putting these two passages together we can see an indication that he created humans as spirit beings. Wrapped up in that spirit is the exact nature of God. God formed the body of man from the dust of the ground and breathed into that body, and the man became a living soul. "Soul" refers to the life of a human being. The Bible mentions that when a person dies, their soul departs from them, meaning they no longer have "breath-life" in them.

Having this foundational understanding of how human beings came to be, we may contemplate, *What is our purpose for being born?* The Book of Revelation informs us, "You are worthy, O Lord our God, to receive glory and honor and power. For you created all things, and they exist because you created what you pleased."[3]

Our purpose is to have a love connection and relationship with our Creator, God, who is Spirit. God created Adam and Eve for his pleasure and clothed them in honor and glory, and he deeply desired fellowship with his created beings. The garden of Eden was God's perfect place to cultivate a loving, trusting relationship with his created ones.

God ruled his creation out of his nature of light, kindness, generosity, selflessness and love. God is love and the true nature of love is giving. Love is at the opposite end of the spectrum from selfishness. God does not withhold his love but intensely desires to express it by sharing his benevolent nature with all of creation.

Furthermore, Adam and Eve were commissioned as God's first ambassadors. They represented his nature to their province: the earth. He blessed them and delegated stewardship and rulership over all their dominion. With that authority came the decree to be fruitful, increase in number, and replenish and subdue the earth. They were to co-rule with God, emanating his nature of love from the garden of Eden. Their relationship with him was perfect. They were created and designed to be dependent upon him for everything.

Genesis establishes God as the intelligent design behind human beings. I have a friend who is thrifty yet tries to be innovative when it comes to eating meals while traveling. One time, while attending a conference at a hotel, he thought he'd save money by getting a frozen burrito and pizza from a local grocery store instead of ordering room service or eating at a restaurant. Since his hotel room had a small refrigerator, it seemed like a good idea. But when he returned from the store, he realized the room was not equipped with a microwave. Undeterred, he took the iron out of the closet and proceeded to use it to heat his burrito. As it sizzled on the iron, the bean filling suddenly exploded! His burrito ruined, he opted for the pizza and decided to string together several paper clips, hook them onto the pizza and then hang it on an outdoor propane heater. As the pizza warmed up, it expanded causing it to plop onto the ground into a gooey mess. Through his efforts, my well-meaning (but still hungry) friend learned that neither the iron nor the propane heater were designed for cooking—just like a microwave is not designed to remove wrinkles from clothes. (Even though I suppose some have tried.)

My friend didn't properly use the resources at hand for what they were truly designed to do. Similarly, if we try going against God's design for us as humans, we will end up with a mess. God created and designed us to depend upon him, and in turn this, dependence produces independence. How? Relationship with God initiates and cultivates trust. Adam and Eve were in union with God as friends and fellow laborers. They were not computers programmed to heartless obedience. They were his image bearers who obeyed out of love.

Trust flourishes where love abounds. The purpose of humankind's existence was to live from a place of intimate communion with God while enjoying his presence and interaction. God gave Adam and Eve freedom of will to make decisions, and their decisions were made in response to God's love. As I contemplated this, I looked out at the lake and then imagined what it must have been like for Adam to walk with God in the cool breeze of the day conversing with him. Life in the garden of Eden never had an "all about me" mindset; it was an "all about God and me" experience under his loving guidance. The prophet Jeremiah wrote, "I know, God, that mere mortals can't run their own lives, That men and women don't have what it takes to take charge of life."[4]

God created and designed us to depend upon him, and in turn, dependence produces independence.

Of all God's creation, only human beings were invited into this relationship of submission, reliance and dependence upon their Creator. The garden of Eden was the perfect manifestation of God's heart. This paradise was like heaven on earth. It was a peaceful environment

Trust flourishes where love abounds.

with pure air to breathe, thirst-quenching water to drink and fresh food that invigorated the body and soul with health. Lush beauty abounded everywhere attracting and pleasing the senses.

Genesis continues to describe the relationship Adam and Eve had with God in the garden. "And they were both naked, the man and his wife, and were not ashamed." This nakedness refers to a child-like innocence. Karl Friedrich Keil and Franz Delitzsch co-authored excellent commentaries on the Old Testament; Keil said Adam and Eve's "souls were arrayed in purity, and their bodies were made holy through the spirit which animated them," while Delitzsch added that they "were naked, but yet they were not so. Their bodies were the clothing of their internal glory; and their internal glory was the clothing of their nakedness." We hear this idea echoed in a Psalm that says of God, "You have clothed him [humanity] in honor and in glory." Adam and Eve were perfect, endowed with illustrious dignity and value.[5] There was no disease or sickness, no poverty or lack, and no knowledge of shame since shame cannot abide where innocence exists. There was only good, but the good included one condition. "And the LORD God commanded the man, saying, 'Of every tree of the garden you may freely eat; but of the tree of the knowledge of good and evil you shall not eat, for in the day that you eat of it you shall surely die.'"[6]

LED UNTO TEMPTATION

As I had another sip of coffee and took in my paradise-like vista, I couldn't imagine a more ideal, stress-free environment than the one that existed at the very beginning. But my pleasant reflection was suddenly interrupted as I realized something happened in the garden. A creature arrived on the scene—and it had a definite bite. Genesis introduces him as the serpent, and Revelation adds, "And the great dragon was thrown down, the serpent of old who is called the devil and Satan." Other titles and characteristics assigned to him throughout the Scripture include: *father of lies, deceiver, accuser, evil one*, and *tempter*.

Most biblical scholars agree that the serpent's story is portrayed by the prophet Isaiah in an epic scene that took place before the creation of the earth, even before the Genesis account. "How you are fallen from heaven, O Lucifer, son of the morning! How you are cut down to the ground—mighty though you were against the nations of the world. For you said to yourself, 'I will ascend to heaven and rule the angels. I will take the highest throne. I will preside on the Mount of Assembly far away in the north. I will climb to the highest heavens and be like the Most High.'"[7] In this passage, Lucifer (the devil) arrogantly professed, "I will" four times, with his final boast aspiring to be like God himself. Pride had overtaken his heart to where he exalted himself above his Creator, claiming independence from God. Later in the Bible, Revelation also records that there was a war in heaven against the devil, who lost the battle and was cast out of heaven with "his angels" (usually referred to as fallen angels or demons).

That is why we find the devil in Genesis 3, there in the garden of Eden disguised as a serpent. He initiated a dialogue with Eve which began to unveil his diabolical intents. "Has God indeed said…?" Compared with various Bible versions, the start of this question could read, "Did God really say?" or "Did God actually say?" The devil's deception began with questioning God's integrity. The devil continued, "You must never eat from any tree of the garden?" Yet that was not what God had said. He actually said, "Of every tree of the garden you may freely eat." Interestingly, God's very first command to humankind was not restrictive, but rather he proclaimed his desired intention of uninhibited abundance. Satan twisted God's statement and removed the word "freely." This was the devil's attempt to distort God's goodness.

The trap was set. Eve was lured with Satan's bait when she considered his question. She responded, "We may eat of the fruit of the trees of the garden, but of the fruit of the tree which is in the midst of the garden, God has said, 'You shall not eat of it, neither shall you touch it, lest ye die.'" Intriguingly, Eve also omitted the word "freely" from God's command and then added a restriction God had never communicated: "neither shall you touch it, lest you die." Eve minimized the word "surely" to "lest," diminishing the certainty of the consequence to only a possibility. Perhaps Eve thought, *If I am not going to die, why would God say that? Maybe he doesn't want me to be like him.* Yet we know God created humankind in his image and likeness. Already, Eve was deceived into seeking wisdom apart from God. Then Satan said to Eve, "You shall not surely die."

Did you catch that? God said, "You shall surely die." The devil said, "You shall not surely die." Eve had a decision to make, one no human had ever considered before. Who was lying? God, or Satan?

The devil continued to systematically contradict God and infect Eve's mind. "For God knows that in the day you eat of it your eyes will be opened, and you will be like God, knowing good and evil." Satan beguiled Eve into choosing independence from and equality to her Creator. She wouldn't die, Satan reassured Eve. She would be as God. Satan also accused God of withholding something potentially great and beneficial from her: the knowledge of good and evil. Obviously, the devil implied, God did not want her or her husband to ascend to his level. God's generous display of goodness to them was not good enough. There was something they were missing. So, as a result of the devil's deception, Adam and Eve took the bait and sinned.[8]

> *Did you catch that? God said, "You shall surely die." The devil said, "You shall not surely die."*

Sin may be defined as seeking for ourselves something which

God did not offer to give us. In essence, Satan implied that God was manipulating Adam and Eve because of God's own selfish interests, while in truth it was the devil who had earlier selfishly declared independence from God, been cast out of heaven, and was now on earth where he had no actual authority. The only power he had was to lie, but a lie has no power unless it is believed.

Anytime we choose self-sufficiency over dependency on God, we set ourselves up not only to be deceived by the devil, but to become his slave. The Bible says, "Don't you realize that you become the slave of whatever you choose to obey?"[9] A selfish "I will" attitude only leads to bondage, which is the opposite of the freedom God offers through loving obedience to him.

Remember, all Adam and Eve knew up until this point was good. God's man and woman were perfectly content. They had everything they needed, including an immediate and intimate spiritual connection with their Creator. They could rely on God for everything: provision for their physical sustenance; contentment in their souls with intellectual and emotional stimulation; and because of the spirit within them, the sustenance of a deep and flourishing fellowship with their Maker. All they had to do was simply trust God. Eve could have ignored the devil or responded to his slander about their Creator by laughing at him and telling him, "What are you, crazy? You have no idea what you're talking about!" Adam, the original recipient of God's commandment regarding the tree of the knowledge of good and evil, could have refuted Eve's claim from the devil. The nature of the devil is to contradict God's will and purposes. His influence on Adam and Eve convinced them that they had the liberty to live apart from God, that they could be self-sufficient without him and that there was something in life greater than simple loving obedience.

> *The only power he had was to lie, but a lie has no power unless it is believed.*

20

Stress is an indicator of the presence of temptation to do something other than God's perfect will. Giving in to that temptation further exacerbates the extent of stress. The first temptation of humankind emerged from an invitation to decide who to believe. That temptation introduced stress when the choice of *whose* will to follow was required. Prior to this encounter with Satan, there had been no stress. Stress first entered the garden of Eden (and the domain of human hearts) when the devil tempted Eve. The origin of stress was birthed in humans with the temptation to depart from the will of God. The first couple did not realize it, but yielding to that temptation would lead to sin and worsen the effects of stress. Submitting to this temptation (of excluding God and obeying a voice other than his) initiated stress for the very first time. Stress increased its momentum, both for Adam and Eve, and then eventually all humanity to come. The Epistle of Romans reveals, "When Adam sinned, the entire world was affected. Sin entered human experience, and death was the result. And so death followed this sin, casting its shadow over all humanity, because all have sinned."[10]

But much, much more was lost that day. When Adam and Eve chose to disobey God and eat of the fruit of the tree of the knowledge of good and evil, it wasn't their bodies or souls that died, but rather their spirits. This connection to their Creator was severed in that precise moment. Without spirit, their lives were limited to the observations and experiences being filtered through the lenses of their five senses. Their created image depreciated into just body and soul. Moreover, this body and soul, originally eternal through spirit-life, would eventually die. God designed human beings with the body subservient to the soul, the soul to the spirit, and the spirit to God. The soul coordinates information from the Spirit of God with the five senses thereby interfacing the inner part of human beings with their physical surroundings. Human innateness includes emotions, thoughts, logic, reasoning, and will. The soul integrates all of these inherent aspects and processes, and through freedom of will determines what governs the heart. Eve decided to eat the fruit because she "saw that the fruit of the tree was good for food and pleasing to the eye, and also desirable for gaining wisdom."[11] She allowed her soul to usurp its subjection to the spirit and ultimately to God. After Adam and Eve lost their spiritual connection, their souls primarily depended on what they saw, heard, touched, tasted and smelled. Their five senses replaced the Spirit of God sitting on the throne of their hearts. Each subsequent generation inherited the fallen nature of Adam.

Adam and Eve had only experienced good and innocence. As a consequence of their disobedience, they indeed became aware of evil. They had once been endued with honor and glory, but their nakedness now revealed their lack of clothing. The new-felt emotions of shame and guilt were discovered, intensifying their stress even further. They began the process of making their own coverings to hide their nakedness in response to these new feelings. This was their first act of walking in their own self-dependence and independence from God. Adam and Eve were originally designed to be the glory of God, but the acceptance of Satan's lie now led them into self-worship and self-service instead. And the tragedy continued.

"In the cool of the evening, the man and his wife heard the Lord God walking around in the garden. So they hid from the Lord God among the trees in the garden. The Lord God called to the man and asked him, 'Where are you?' He answered, 'I heard you in the garden. I was afraid because I was naked, so I hid.' God asked, 'Who told you that you were naked? Did you eat fruit from the tree I commanded you not to eat from?' The man answered, 'That woman, the one you gave me, gave me some fruit from the tree, and I ate it.' Then the Lord God asked the woman, 'What have you done?' 'The snake deceived me, and I ate,' the woman answered."[12]

Adam and Eve went from enjoying the presence of God in the cool breeze of the day to being afraid of him. When they heard God's voice, they hid themselves. Adam also blamed God for giving him the woman who, he said, caused him to disobey. Fear and blame bubbled up within them, and each new remorseful feeling brought new stress with it. Yet God did not abandon his created ones in their day of disobedience. Instead, he pursued them and asked two very important questions: "Where are you?" and "Who told you?"

God continues to lovingly pursue us and asks us to contemplate these same questions today. His inquiries are not intended to intimidate us, but are designed to gently lead us to a heart of repentance. I know: in today's vernacular, the word *repentance* is an abused religious expression. In its best usage it simply means for one to change direction for a better outcome. God does not overstep our freedom of will, but he certainly does not leave us alone either. He extends a continuous invitation to walk with him. To begin that journey, God desires us to acknowledge what Adam and Eve did not. When we repent, we say, "I'm sorry for rejecting your counsel and hiding from you. So, where do we go from here?" When we apologize to him and then answer those questions, we are repositioned to have the stresses in our lives (including shame, guilt, fear and blame) removed by the forgiveness of God.

Sin causes us to become afraid of God. It is in that state where we find it hard to trust that God really means what he says, and that he will really do what he says he will do. Therefore, we try to hide from our Creator because we are self-conscious and ashamed of sin in our lives. We realize our paradise has been shattered. Perhaps we should ask ourselves, "Where am I in my relationship with God? Am I slowly drifting apart from his goodness and love? Am I trying to hide something from him?" The second thing we might ask ourselves is, "Who told me what God said? Who is attempting to introduce things that contradict God's true perspective and undermine my ability to trust in him?"

Stress, then, results from the pressure of dealing with temptation and the consequences of yielding to that temptation. God did not design us to be constantly under stress. It is only through him that we can find help to alleviate and eliminate stress from our lives. Where then, precisely, does this help come from? Many Scriptures begin to reveal the answer through the lives of biblical characters. They were real people, "whoevers" like you and me, who dealt with real stress.

References

1.   Genesis 1:31a (NLT)

2.   Genesis 2:18 (TLB)

3.   Revelation 4:11 (NLT)

4.   Jeremiah 10:23 (MSG)

5.   Genesis 2:25; Biblical Commentary on the Old Testament, by Carl Friedrich Keil and Franz Delitzsch [1857-78]. Text Courtesy of Internet Sacred Texts Archive and Psalm 8:5b (ABPE)

6.   Genesis 2:16-17

7.   Isaiah 14:12-14 (TLB)

8.   Narrative based on various translations of Genesis 3:1-5

9.   Romans 6:16a (NLT)

10.   Romans 5:12 (TPT)

11.   Genesis 3:6 (NLV)

12.   Genesis 3:8-13 (GW)

CHAPTER 3

GOING FROM LIMITED TO LIMITLESS

I watched my mother pack my bathing suit, my favorite red-hooded sweatshirt, and a towel into a gym bag. Anticipation surged in my soul. Our family was leaving to visit some friends who owned a horse farm with a spring-fed swimming pond.

Upon our arrival, my siblings and I said a polite, Hello, and then restlessly waited while our parents and friends chit-chatted for what seemed like forever. Finally, our perceptive hostess asked us, would you like to go swimming? Like lightning, we were off to the changing room to jump into our swimsuits. We raced to the water and happily skipped into the shallow part of the pond. Our parents kept an eye on us, calling from the distance not to go too far into the water. We complied, and all was well. After our swim my brother and sisters headed back into the house to warm up, but I chose to stay outdoors. I donned my favorite sweatshirt, pulled the hood over my wet head and allowed the sun to take the chill out of my shivering body.

The persistent neighing of the horses drew my attention to the corral, so I went over to get a closer look. I whistled, hoping to coax them over to the fence, but the horses were more interested in eating the fresh hay strewn about the feeding trough. Unable to make contact with my equine friends, I turned my back on them and casually leaned against the fence to face the distant pond. Suddenly, my view changed dramatically! I realized I was being elevated off the ground because a horse had snuck up behind me and grabbed my hood in his mouth. As I was lifted up, the sweatshirt tightened around my neck! I frantically tried to let out a scream, but it was silenced by my constricted throat. My mind raced. *Am I going to be hanged by a horse? My life has been too short! What a way to go!* As my vision blurred, I summoned from within a desperate prayer to God: *Help!*

Though the sounds were muffled by the pounding in my ears, I heard footsteps rapidly approaching and voices shouting. My dad yanked my hood from the horses jaws. I gasped for air as I fell into my father's arms.

"Help" is a simple but effective prayer. There are many stressful situations and circumstances in which we find ourselves helpless. *Where* do we turn when no remedy is on the horizon? Does God really *hear* our pleas? If so, *when* does he respond? Are there factors that *hinder* his response? Finally, what happens as a *result* of his response?

WHERE DO WE GO FOR HELP?

The Psalms declare, "I look up to the mountains and hills, longing for God's help. But then I realize that our true help and protection come only from the Lord, our Creator who made the heavens and the earth."[1] The mountains and hills in this passage refer to Mount Zion, the location of the temple of God, the dwelling place of the presence of the Lord. It represented the *God Place* for those to whom this Psalm was written. The word help includes assistance, aid, strength, provision and healing.

While in India on a mission trip, I observed people praying to the hills that surrounded their villages. In those hills were many temples, also the homes of their gods. People believe that by looking up to their gods in prayer, they will receive help. The psalmist, though, boldly announced that his help comes from the one true God who made heaven and earth.

The Psalms often encourage us to look for help from the Lord. They renew our hearts and fill us with fresh hope. Here's a small sampling of some of these declarations.

"Our soul waits for the LORD; He is our help and our shield." Waiting for the Lord means to look him with expectation, and intertwine our hearts with his promises. The shield represents defense, protection and safety. "Because you are my helper, I sing for joy in the shadow of your wings." This passage illustrates God's watchful care through the imagery of a mother hen extending her wings over her young chicks. It portrays a rejoicing heart filled with confidence, rest and peace.

"Help" is a simple but effective prayer.

Another encouraging verse is, "You who fear the LORD, trust in the LORD; He is their help and their shield." Whenever we read the word "fear" in the New King James Version and most other translations, there are two possible definitions. It either means *to be afraid* or *to have awe, reverence and respect.* The context determines the meaning. This verse refers to having awe, reverence and respect for God. This how we begin placing our trust in him. That is why the Psalms admonish, "We can never look to men for help; no matter who they are, they can't save us, for even our great leaders fail and fall. They too are just mortals who will one day die. At death the spirits of all depart and their bodies return to dust. In the day of their death all their projects and plans are over. But those who hope in the Lord will be happy and pleased! Our help comes from the God of Jacob!" The Psalms say twice, "Give us help from trouble, For the help of man is useless." Does this mean people cannot aid us in our stress? The understanding rests upon the importance of first seeking help from God. Allow him to give direction as to what to do. It may involve others; it may not. Compared to God's infinite wisdom and resources, people are insufficient. Remember, we are designed to primarily pursue our Creator. Without him, our attempts to remedy stress are futile compared to his divine intervention in our time of need. "Know that the LORD, He is God; It is He who has made us, and not we ourselves; We are His people and the sheep of His pasture."[2]

DOES GOD HEAR WHEN WE CALL OUT FOR HELP?

In the Psalms we find this promise from God: "Because he holds fast to me in love, I will deliver him; I will protect him, because he knows my name. When he calls to me, I will answer him; I will be with him in trouble; will rescue him and honor him." Did you notice how love is mentioned first? Determine right now that God is love and in love with you! The First Epistle of John reveals that we love him because he first loved us. When we respond to God's love with our love, our loving response releases God's powerful resources to help us. He promises to answer us, deliver us, set us on high, honor us and be with us during our stress as we set our love on him and call upon him (ask for help). This interaction of love all begins by going to the *God Place*.

The psalmist explains why he loves God. "I love God because he listened to me, listened as I begged for mercy. He listened so intently as I laid out my case before him. Death stared me in the face; hell was hard on my heels. Up against it, I didn't know which way to turn; then I called out to God for help: 'Please, God!' I cried out. 'Save my life!' God is gracious—it is he who makes things right, our most compassionate God. God takes the side of the helpless; when I was at the end of my rope, he saved me." Words and phrases in the Scriptures such as *listen, hear, give ear, give heed, incline his ear, hearken, answer,* and *respond* all have related meanings. Knowing this brings the understanding that when God

With billions of "whoevers" occupying the planet, God's attentive ear is always listening for the heart-cry of just one soul.

28

hears, it means he *answers*. But you may wonder, *Why would God listen to me?* Because he knows all about you; the good, the bad and everything in between—yet he is still unconditionally and fervently in love with you!

How awesome it is to think about God's unfathomable love. With billions of "whoevers" occupying the planet, God's attentive ear is always listening for the heart-cry of just one soul. Whenever he is beckoned, he immediately sweeps over the entire population and pinpoints the one calling out unto him. Then, with wide-open arms, he tenderly embraces that very individual with affectionate attentiveness.

These extended excerpts from Psalm 139 expound God's limitless, never-ending love for us as he hears and answers our personal pleas for help.

"Lord, you know everything there is to know about me. You've examined my innermost being with your loving gaze. You perceive every movement of my heart and soul, and understand my every thought before it even enters my mind. You are so intimately aware of me, Lord. You read my heart like an open book and you know all the words I'm about to speak before I even start a sentence! You know every step I will take before my journey even begins! You've gone into my future to prepare the way, and in kindness you follow behind me to spare me from the harm of my past. With your hand of love upon my life, you impart a Father's blessing to me."

"You formed my innermost being, shaping my delicate inside and my intricate outside, and wove them all together in my mother's womb. I thank you, God, for making me so mysteriously complex! It simply amazes me to think about it! How thoroughly you know me Lord! You even formed every bone in my body when you created me in the secret place; carefully, skillfully shaping me

29

from nothing to something."

"Every single moment you are thinking of me! How precious and wonderful to consider that you cherish me constantly in your every thought! O God, your desires toward me are more than the grains of sand on every shore! When I awake each morning, you're still thinking of me."

This Psalm reveals why God hears and answers us when we cry out to him. He loves us and passionately wants to connect with us in an intimate relationship thus guiding us deeper into the immeasurable grandeur of the *God Place.*[3]

WHEN DOES HE RESPOND?

There is a pattern revealed in the Scriptures regarding God's response to our stress. As noted in Chapter 1, distress and trouble are mentioned in the Scriptures in the context of God responding to you in "the day of distress" or "the time of trouble." These situations can refer to a twenty-four hour period, a portion of a day or a season of time, depending upon the context.

I was once in Mexico helping to start a *God Place* fellowship in a man's home. We went to a huge city market and walked for miles through aisle after aisle of merchants. We took in the displays of bright colorful fabrics, listened to the bustling sounds of negotiating, and inhaled the tantalizing aromas of freshly prepared food. After several hours, we decided to go to a nearby park to rest. We sat on a bench by a large fountain and under the shade of tall trees. A young boy skipped happily around the fountain as his mother enjoyed the innocent playfulness of her son. Suddenly, the boy tripped, fell and scraped his knee. His laughter was abruptly silenced, followed only seconds later by the familiar cry, "Mama!" She responded instantly, swept him into her arms and soothed him until his wailing was reduced to a soft whimper.

My thoughts went to God. He created little ones with the natural urge to cry out for help when in need. Children instinctively know where to run for relief, and as parents we have an inner predisposition to respond to a child's cry. The prophet Isaiah reveals God saying, "Can a woman forget her nursing child, And not have compassion on the son of her womb? Surely they may forget, Yet I will not forget you. See, I have inscribed you on the palms of My hands; Your walls are continually before Me." Even though parents sometimes abandon their children, God will *never* neglect us. He has "inscribed" us upon the tenderest portion of his hands so that we are always in his sight and remembrance.

The Psalms affirm, "All who are oppressed may come to him. He is a refuge for them in their times of trouble. All those who know your mercy, Lord, will count on you for help. For you have never yet forsaken those who trust in you." In our times of stress, our natural response should be to run to our *God Place*, and leap into the protecting, loving arms of our heavenly Father—just like the child who scraped his knee. God's response is to come to our rescue and soothe us. He is our place of refuge in time of need. As we deepen our relationship with him, our reflexes will improve so that we will habitually run to him and expect his deliverance.[4]

Jesus always spoke the words that his Father revealed to him, and many times it was through a parable: a figure of speech drawing a parallel between two dissimilar things. One interesting parable explains that we should always pray to God and not give up in times of stress.

"There was once a judge in some city who never gave God a thought and cared nothing for people. A widow in that city kept after him: 'My rights are being violated. Protect me!' He never gave her the time of day. But after this went on and on he said to himself, 'I care nothing what God thinks, even less what people think. But because this widow won't quit badgering me,

I'd better do something and see that she gets justice-otherwise I'm going to end up beaten black-and-blue by her pounding.' Then the Master said, "Do you hear what that judge, corrupt as he is, is saying? So what makes you think God won't step in and work justice for his chosen people, who continue to cry out for help? Won't he stick up for them? I assure you, he will. He will not drag his feet."

The two dissimilar points in this parable are an unjust judge who *did not* want to listen to a widow, and God who *does* listen and who *swiftly* vindicates his own. Again the Psalms confirm that God will not drag his feet: "Listen to my prayer, O LORD, and hear my cry for help! When I am in trouble, don't turn away from me! Listen to me, and answer me quickly when I call . . . He will hear his forsaken people and listen to their prayer . . . God is 'a very present help' in times of trouble." [5]

Sometimes our day of distress is self-inflicted. One psalm of David declares, "Please be willing, O LORD, to rescue me! O LORD, hurry and help me . . . I am oppressed and needy! May the LORD pay attention to me! You are my helper and my deliverer! O my God, do not delay!"[6] Scholars believe David spoke this prayer for help when unspecified troubles abounded in his life because of his sin and the gloating of his enemies that resulted from his sin. When we willfully disobey God or engage in an activity we know conflicts with his will, stress ensues. But we do not need to stay in that state. If we have failed God, we can call to him as David did. He will not delay; he will move quickly with urgent haste to unleash the powerful resources of heaven.

God will also respond when our time of trouble is brought on by an enemy. David proclaimed, "I call to you in times of trouble [the day of my distress], because you will answer me." Bible experts believe that his prayer for help resulted from an attack by enemies, whose fierce onslaughts reflected their disdain for the Lord God.

In Africa, the people have this expression. "You tell us we kill one another with weapons, but in America, you kill one another with words." It's easy to feel threatened or even defeated by the words of others. James wrote, "You want what you don't have, so you scheme and kill to get it. You are jealous of what others have, but you can't get it, so you fight and wage war to take it away from them. Yet you don't have what you want because you don't ask God for it." He was not talking about the physical act of killing. Rather, this verse refers to envy and anger depicted by cruel words and vengeful acts to another. Left unchecked, these root causes (when nurtured) lead to killing. There's no doubt words may be injurious but God will hear and help when others have wounded us with their slanderous remarks.[7]

In fact, it's best to prepare ourselves for battle *every day*. David prayerfully declared, "The Lord will answer you in times of trouble. The name of the God of Jacob will protect you." He will send you help from his holy place."[8] This prayer was also offered by others on behalf of those going out into battle. Even one in the position of king or queen is not immune from the day of trouble. Everyone needs help from God. It is remarkable to think that regardless of David's all-consuming schedule as both king and warrior, he devoted time for God. We don't need to begin our day by rushing about. We should develop the habit of going to our *God Place* and proactively requesting help in anticipation of whatever comes our way. This may be done privately or by participating with others. Either way, we can prepare our hearts and have confidence that God will cause us to be victorious.

Finally, praise is a vital aspect of asking God for help: praising him in advance for his response in the good and bad times. It is a great way to exercise our faith in him. Then, when God comes to our rescue, we will want to praise him even more. God gives this invitation and says, "Call to me when trouble comes; I will save you, and you will praise me." Our response can be like David's. "But I will sing of your strength; I will sing aloud of your steadfast love in the morning. For you have been to me a fortress and a refuge in the day of my distress. O my Strength, I will sing praises to you, for you, O God, are my fortress, the God who shows me steadfast love. In this passage, the usage of "fortress" speaks of a place of protection such as an impenetrable fort set high on a hill, while "refuge" comes from the root word for "flight" and portrays a way of escaping to safety. These descriptions help us to define the *God Place*.[9]

It is an interesting insight, that often, our refuge is where we run to in times of distress or trouble. That is normal and usually referred to as the "fight or flight" response (a reaction to a perceived threat by our sympathetic nervous system). With the mere perception of danger, the medulla in our brain and our adrenal glands automatically release two stress hormones, adrenaline and norepinephrine. These messengers cause our blood vessels to constrict, muscles to tighten, nerve endings to heighten, heartbeat to increase and lungs to breathe heavier. Stress hormones actually prepare the body to fight the danger or run from it. A third hormone, cortisol, is subsequently released to help adapt and mobilize these responses, reseting the body and mind back to a pre-stress state.

I recall the time God somehow got my attention to find a refuge when I was on the run from him. I had drifted away from asking him for help and was slowly growing deaf to his voice. Working hard to try and solve problems on my own, I didn't have much to show for all my efforts. At that time, I tended to blame God, assuming he didn't care. Yet I knew in the depth of my heart that I was really the one at fault. As a last resort, I flew to Tucson, Arizona, to attend a conference about connecting with God. Because of my financial status, I stayed at a budget motel. What a mistake that was! The wallpaper was peeling, the shower persistently leaked, and the guests in the next room were having a ruckus that elicited the barking of their dogs. In my emotionally irritated state, I felt as though my life was slowly draining away.

The first day of the conference a speaker talked about one

particular lesson Jesus taught. It pertained to God providing considerable care to the birds of the air and the flowers of the field and how much greater his care was for his own children. (We will devote some time to those passages later in the book.) Another insight from the conference was how God was a fountain of living water.

Both ideas became more than academic knowledge for me that day. After the session, a friend and I went for a hike in the desert. We came across a cistern. It was dry, cracked and full of tumbleweeds and reptiles. A cistern is used to collect and store rain water. During biblical times, cisterns were dug out of a large rock. Many times these rocks developed cracks and the water slowly leaked out. The prophet Jeremiah, speaking on God's behalf, referred to a cistern. "For my people have done two evil things: They have abandoned me—the fountain of living water. And they have dug for themselves cracked cisterns that can hold no water at all!" God was deeply concerned that "his people" were ignoring him, who is the endless life-source of fresh water, and relying instead on their own stagnant self-efforts and limited resources. God emphatically called this evil.[10]

As I peered into that desert cistern, God spoke to my heart for what seemed to be the first time in many years. He said, "If you want to live a budget motel lifestyle, keep trying to do everything in your own strength." He then instructed me to check out of the motel and get another room at a nearby resort. I could hardly believe what he was instructing me to do. "Do you mean like a luxury hotel?" I asked. "Yes," God reassured me. "Don't worry! I'll provide." I followed through on God's direction and discovered a beautiful place in the foothills of Tucson's Santa Catalina Mountains. As I pulled into the resort's long driveway, my heart rejoiced as I saw rows of beautiful flowers. Birds were singing and cheerfully swooping in and out of the trees, and arbors of flowering plants tastefully adorned the property. Driving up to the lobby, a flowing fountain greeted me at the entrance, and I thought of God, the fountain of living water. The Lord God spoke to my heart once again. "If you let me handle your problems, you can live a resort lifestyle instead of a budget motel one." I entered the hotel, and was immediately engulfed by its lush atmosphere of peace and comfort. The front desk manager enthusiastically welcomed me, upgraded my room to a suite at no extra charge, and told me there was a promotion going on. Room prices were a mere fifteen dollars more per night than the budget motel. This blissful haven was quiet and clean; the friendly staff attended to every need. There were swimming pools and hot tubs all situated near the breathtaking views of the mountains.

I slept peacefully and soundly that night and woke up refreshed early the next morning. The temperature was brisk outside, so I put on the spa robe provided in my room and headed to the hot tub, anticipating a glorious sunrise over the mountains. Caressed by the warm water comforting me in the chilly air, I listened to the birds sing their morning symphony. Taking in the newness of day, I watched the sunlight illuminate colorful arrays of flowers one after another.

This elegant hotel became a sanctuary, a place to "resort" to and commune once again with my Creator, the God who called himself my heavenly Father. I had discovered the *God Place*! My prayer and confession was like the psalmist's. "I run for dear life to God, I'll never live to regret it. Do what you do so well: get me out of this mess and up on my feet. Put your ear to the ground and listen, give me space for salvation. Be a guest room where I can retreat; you said your door was always open! You're my salvation—my vast, granite fortress."[11]

ARE THERE FACTORS THAT HINDER GOD'S RESPONSE?

Ever since sin entered the world in the garden of Eden, there has been a void within human beings. From the depths of the Amazon rainforest to the peaks of the Himalayas, every culture has displayed some expression of innate hunger and gravitation toward something they call "divine" in order to fill that emptiness. We have fashioned gods and all sorts of doctrines and rituals to worship and appease those gods. Even God's chosen people, the children of Israel, were often distracted from their Creator. Israel turned to worship idols, first in their thoughts, then in their hearts and finally with outwardly formed images to stimulate and remind them of their gods. While not all stress is a result of idolatry, the practice of idolatry, setting something before God's face, leads to stressful situations and circumstances.

The very first commandment God gave the children of Israel concerned idolatry. "You shall have no other gods before Me." The Hebrew text renders this passage *before my face or in front of my presence*. Right now, look at an object or a person across from you, then cup your hands together directly in front of your face. Even though the object or person is still present, you have put something before it or them. God expects nothing to come between his face and ours. Anything placed before him becomes an idol that draws people away from the helping presence of the Lord. David wrote, "When You said, 'Seek My face,' My heart said to You, 'Your face, LORD, I will seek. Do not hide Your face from me; Do not turn Your servant away in anger; You have been my help; Do not leave me nor forsake me, O God of my salvation.'" The word *face* represents the intimate presence of God. He wants us to seek his presence.

Seeking is not a passive activity. It is a heartfelt response of thankfulness to his love. A chief musician of the temple wrote, "Why are you in despair, my soul? Why are you disturbed within me? Hope in God! For I shall still praise him for the saving help of his presence." When we are discouraged and lacking peace, we can seek the presence of the Lord and expect to experience intimacy with him. This again helps us outline the purposeful meaning of the *God Place*.[12]

The Book of Nehemiah records a time when the children of Israel were led into the land God had promised to them, yet they still turned their hearts away from him.

"And they captured fortified cities and a rich land, and took possession of houses full of all good things, cisterns already hewn, vineyards, olive orchards and fruit trees in abundance. So they ate and were filled and became fat and delighted themselves in your great goodness. Nevertheless, they were disobedient and rebelled against you and cast your law behind their back and killed your prophets, who had warned them in order to turn them back to you, and they committed great blasphemies. Therefore you gave them into the hand of their enemies, who made them suffer. And in the time of their suffering they cried out to you and you heard them from heaven, and according to your great mercies you gave them saviors who saved them from the hand of their enemies. But after they had rest they did evil again before you, and you abandoned them to the hand of their enemies, so that they had dominion over them. Yet when they turned and cried to you, you heard from heaven, and many times you delivered them according to your mercies."

Even though God prospered the children of Israel, they became disobedient and rebellious. They arrogantly turned their backs on God's loving instructions and even murdered his prophets, those specifically sent to turn their hearts back to him. Hardship and stress resulted from their choice to forsake God, but when they cried to him for help, he delivered them. Yet their repentance was short lived. When they continued to embrace idolatry, it finally led them to captivity. Even worse, they became servants in their own land. The consequences were disheartening. "Behold, we are slaves this day; in the land that you gave to our fathers to enjoy its fruit and its good gifts, behold, we are slaves. And its rich yield goes to the kings whom you have set over us because of our sins. They rule over our bodies and over our livestock as they please, and we are in great distress."[13]

The Book of Judges tells another story of idolatrous woe, but with a twist.

"Finally the Israelis turned to Jehovah again and begged him to save them. 'We have sinned against you and have forsaken you as our God and have worshiped idols,' they confessed. But the Lord replied, 'Didn't I save you from the Egyptians, the Amorites, the Ammonites, the Philistines, the Sidonians, the Amalekites, and the Maonites? Has there ever been a time when you cried out to me that I haven't rescued you? Yet you continue to abandon me and to worship other gods. So go away; I won't save you anymore. Go and cry to the new gods you have chosen! Let them save you in your hour of distress!' But they pleaded with him again and said, 'We have sinned. Punish us in any way you think best, only save us once more from our enemies.' Then they destroyed their foreign gods and worshiped only the Lord; and he was grieved by their misery."[14]

The children of Israel were serving other gods and idols. God strongly suggested that the Israelites cry out to those gods which they had chosen and to let those idols deliver them in their time of stress. Of course, God knew how that was going to work out for them. He wanted them to realize that he was their only possible source of help. Seeking help from things other than God is always a choice we can make, but never a wise one.

Idols may sometimes be physical objects but they are always set up in the heart. They become a "stumbling block" that will trip us up every time. However, our assurance from God is that no matter how far we turn away from him, if we cry out to him he will bring us back. We are never beyond the reach of God's help. But we must put away anything that has been an idol in our lives-anything! Even fashioning our own *God Place* and embellishing a physical atmosphere with pleasurable attributes may develop into a substitute for God himself!

There was a time in my life not so long ago when the Bible became my idol. As disturbing, blasphemous or uncomfortable as that may sound, I esteemed and elevated the study of the Scriptures so much that I eagerly sought its direction and counsel above the fresh and present voice of God. While relying on my *knowledge* of the book more than my *relationship* with its author, I was determined to habitually look up the Hebrew and Greek definitions of scriptural terms and trust in my own insights instead of seeking God's wisdom. My focus was more on reading than prayer, and on definitions of words rather than the true meaning behind them. Just like the record of Jeremiah 2:13, I had forsaken the one who was the supply of living water and through my own efforts, fashioned out a broken cistern. It was filled with academic knowledge, yet I was lacking an intimate relationship with my Creator and the blessings that flow from that experience. But then God graciously revealed that even a resource as vast and treasure-packed as the Bible could not help me apart from his active involvement and participation.

> *"I called on the Lord in my distress. I cried to my God for help. He heard my voice from his temple, and my cry for help reached his ears. He brought me out to a wide-open place. He rescued me because he was pleased with me."*

With his help, I learned to put away my reliance on that self-imposed idol and instead sought God as my primary source for help. I gladly embraced these words from the Psalms: "You are my strength and my shield from every danger. When I fully trust in you, help is on the way. I jump for joy and burst forth with ecstatic, passionate praise! I will sing songs of what you mean to me!"[15] Do you notice the upward cycle? Recognizing God as our strength and shield builds trust in him. Then we are able to receive his help. As a result, our hearts will rejoice and we will sing his praises. This praise will fortify within us a confidence that God will empower and watch over us and cause our lives to spiral upward to a greater relationship with him as our help.

WHAT HAPPENS AS A RESULT OF HIS RESPONSE?

Have you imagined the oppression that heroes like Gandhi, Mandela, Brother Yun, and the apostles Paul and Peter endured as they were confined to prison? What exhilaration they must have experienced when their cell doors were opened and they were finally set free. Yet there are other prisons beside physical places of incarceration. There are also prisons of our secret sins we dare not share with anybody. We may be shackled to some trauma from our past, or there may be other unresolved problems that still plague our lives. But when we call out to God for help, he promises to set us free.

One way God responds to our pleas for help is by relieving our stress. The Scriptures use the concept of "enlarging" to illustrate God's intervention. David declared this. "God, you are my righteousness, my champion defender. Answer me when I cry for help! Whenever I was in distress, you enlarged me. I'm being squeezed again—I need your kindness right away! Grant me your grace, hear my prayer, and set me free!" We already know that stress is like an ever-tightening constriction and a troubling pressure. To "enlarge" means to *free, relieve,* or *open into a roomy pasture.* David adds this further insight. "I called on the Lord in my distress. I cried to my God for help. He heard my voice from his temple, and my cry for help reached his ears. He brought me out to a wide-open place. He rescued me because he was pleased with me."[16]

When we are stressed, we should call upon the Lord. He will hear our voice and answer. Our cry for help will not go in one ear and out the other. He will deliver us and lead us into a spacious place because he is pleased with us. Another translation says, "He delights in us." "Delight" means to *incline towards with pleasure.* Imagine God leaning toward you with great delight and cupping his hand around his ear in order to listen to your prayer, closely and with devotion. Then imagine the Lord rescuing you from your stress and leading you from a confining situation into a spacious place of deliverance and freedom.

This "wide-open place" referred to by David, reminds me of the twenty-third Psalm.

"The Lord is my best friend and my shepherd. I always have more than enough. He offers a resting place for me in his luxurious love. His tracks take me to an oasis of peace, the quiet brook of bliss. That's where he restores and revives my life. He opens before me pathways to God's pleasure and leads me along in his footsteps of righteousness so that I can bring honor to his name. Lord, even when your path takes me through the valley of deepest darkness, fear will never conquer me, for you already have! You remain close to me and lead me through it all the way. Your authority is my strength and my peace. The comfort of your love takes away my fear. I'll never be lonely, for you are near. You become my delicious feast even when my enemies dare to fight. You anoint me with the fragrance of your Holy Spirit; you give me all I can drink of you until my heart overflows. So why would I fear the future? For your goodness and love pursue me all the days of my life. Then afterward, when my life is through, I'll return to your glorious presence to be forever with you!"[17]

This, my friend, paints a picture of what the *God Place* can be for you!

Another Psalm asserts, "In my distress I cried out to the Lord. The Lord answered me and put me in a wide open place. The Lord is on my side, I am not afraid! What can people do to me?"[18] Again, the Bible reveals a recognizable pattern: when we are stressed, we can call upon the Lord and he will hear and answer us and relieve our stress. A relationship of reliance on God blossoms into a continually growing confidence and trust where we will confess, "The Lord is on my side, I am not afraid! What can people do to me?"

Perhaps some of you are drowning in debt or trapped in an abusive relationship. Maybe you are imprisoned by an addiction or experiencing an unexpected emotional storm that is raging in your life. I urge you to look in the mirror and then think about what Isaiah wrote. "You have been a refuge for the poor, a refuge for the needy in their distress, a shelter from the storm and a shade from the heat. For the breath of the ruthless is like a storm driving against a wall." The "breath of the ruthless" and "storm driving against the wall" are idioms of expression where relentless winds and stormy circumstances seem to be pounding against our lives. Don't give up! Determine right now that you are going to go to God and receive his help. He will hear and answer your cry. He is intimately and deeply in love with *you* and wants to help *you* move from the limited place to the limitless *God Place*. God is faithful; he promises to rescue you from your stress and lead you to a place where you will revel in newfound freedom. Come out from your shackles and be led into the wide-open pasture of his faithful promises to you. Then you will also proclaim like the psalmist, "Return to your rest, O my soul, For the Lord has dealt bountifully with you."[19]

The Bible is filled with stories of people who faced incredible stress, often more intense than anything we have experienced. In the next few chapters we will examine the accounts of several "whoevers" (those who sought God during their days of distress), and discover how he delivered them.

References

1.   Psalm 121:1-2 (TPT)

2.   Psalm 33:20 (NASB); Psalm 63:7 (NLT); Psalm 115:11; Psalm 146:3-5 (TPT); Psalm 60:11; 108:12 and Psalm 100:3

3.   Psalm 91:14-15 (ESV); 1 John 4:19; Psalm 116:1-6 (MSG) and Psalm 139:1-4, 13-15, 17-18 (TPT)

4.   Isaiah 49:15 and 16; Psalms 9:9 and 10 (TLB)

5.   Luke 18:2-8a (MSG); Psalm 102:1, 2 and 17 (GNT) and Psalm 46:1 (KJV)

6.   Psalm 40:13 and 17 and mirrored in Psalm 70:1 and 5 (NET)

7.   Psalm 86:7 (EXB) and James 4:2 (NLT)

8.   Psalm 20:1-2a (GW)

9.   Psalm 50:15 (GNT) and Psalm 59:16 and 17 (ESV)

10. Matthew 6:25-29 and Jeremiah 2:13 (NLT)

11. Psalm 71:1-3 (MSG)

12. Exodus 20:3; Psalm 27:8 and 9 and Psalm 42:5 (WEB)
13. Nehemiah 9:25-28 (ESV) and Nehemiah 9:36 and 37 (ESV)
14. Judges 10:10-16 (TLB)
15. Psalm 28:7 (TPT)
16. Psalm 4:1 (TPT) and Psalm 18:6, 19 (GW)
17. Psalm 23 (TPT)
18. Psalm 118:5 and 6 (NET)
19. Isaiah 25:4 (NIV) and Psalm 116:7

CHAPTER 4

HOW JACOB WAS RESCUED
FROM STRESS

As told in the Book of Genesis, Jacob was the son of Isaac and Rebekah, the grandson of Abraham and the twin brother of Esau. Jacob's life originated out of a prayer by his father and mother; it also began with immediate conflict.

His mother Rebekah could not conceive a child, but his father Isaac prayed and asked God for help on her behalf, and Rebekah became pregnant. As her pregnancy progressed she felt a struggle within her womb. She grew concerned and asked God what was going on. God replied, "There are two nations in your womb. From birth they will be two rival peoples. One of these peoples will be stronger than the other, and the older will serve the younger." The cultural practice of these times was for the parents to name their newborn with respect to the baby's appearance, a circumstance surrounding the birth, or a special characteristic noted. Sometimes the parents named the baby relating to a desired destiny for the child. When the twins were born, the firstborn came out red and covered with hair. His parents named him Esau, meaning "hairy" and "rough." The second boy came out and grabbed on to the heel of his older brother, so they named him Jacob, meaning "to take by the heel" and "to take the place of another," or "supplanter."

As the boys grew, Esau became a skillful hunter who loved the

45

outdoors, while Jacob was more of the pastoral, quiet type who stayed at home. Isaac loved Esau because of the wild game he brought and served him, but Rebekah loved Jacob. This parental partiality caused stress that eventually brought devastating consequences to the family. One day, as Jacob was cooking a mouthwatering red lentil stew, his brother Esau staggered in from the field faint from hunger. Hardly able to stand, he begged for some of the food. Like a hawk poised to swoop down on his prey, Jacob's cunning heart pounded as he saw an opportune moment to usurp his brother.

"Sell me your birthright now," Jacob insisted. The birthright was enormously significant. Given to the firstborn son, it included the spiritual and physical privileges of a double inheritance, rule over the family in the absence of the father, and in this case, continuation of a promise God had made to Abraham, a promise destined to continue in the family line for generations to come.

Esau's concern with things like birthrights and promises was overshadowed by his craving for immediate gratification. Hysterically he cried out, "Look! I am about to die of starvation! What good is my birthright to me if I am dead?" Jacob calmly sealed the deal by making Esau swear, meaning that if Esau violated the oath, Jacob could take his life. The transaction took place without much contemplation. For a mere morsel of bread and dish of lentils, the birthright became Jacob's. Esau threw away his God-given rights and privileges for a quick fix to a temporary problem. This folly brought more stress into the family, and Esau never sought repentance for his decision, one that constantly seethed in his soul for years. Perhaps Esau's apparent disregard for God's promises was why he later married two Hittite women, descendants of the Canaanites. This act violated the covenant commandment given by God to his grandfather Abraham. These foreign women caused Isaac and Rebekah great anxiety.[1]

Years later, the parents' partiality, plus the ongoing strife between the two brothers, reached a climactic conclusion. Isaac had become old and blind. One day he called upon his favored son.

"Esau, I don't know how many days I have left. Go to the fields and hunt some venison. Prepare it for me the way I love it. Then I will eat it and give you a blessing before I die." Esau's heart must have surged with anticipation, because he knew that this blessing, unlike his squandered birthright, could not be given to just anyone. It was a prophetic last will and testament. It was considered to be treasure from heaven. He departed for the hunt with great expectancy.

Rebekah overheard Isaac talking to Esau and immediately sought to protect her favorite son. She relayed to Jacob what Isaac had requested of his older brother, then said, "My son, obey me now. Go to our flock and bring me two of the best kid goats. I will prepare them just like the flavorful venison that your father loves. Then you can serve your father's favorite dish to him so that he blesses you before he dies." Clearly, Rebekah knew that Isaac's blessing for his beloved Esau would be greater than Jacob's and therefore wanted it instead for her preferred child. She decided to try to help along God's promise of the older serving the younger.

While Jacob didn't have a problem with the lie, he saw a flaw in his mother's plan. He reminded her that Esau was hairy, while he had smooth skin. He knew his father might feel his hands and arms and then realize he was being deceived. Jacob did not want to risk receiving a curse rather than a blessing from his father. "If that happens," Rebekah replied, "let the curse be on me. Now go! Do what I said."

Jacob obeyed, and Rebekah made the meal. Then she took some of Esau's clothing and put them on Jacob, and placed the skins of the goats on Jacob's arms and the back of his neck to simulate Esau's hair. Jacob approached his father.

"Who are you, my son?" Isaac asked.

"I am Esau, your firstborn," Jacob lied. "I have done what you asked of me. Please come, sit and eat of my venison. Then bless me as you have promised."

Isaac wondered how his son had hunted and prepared the venison so quickly. Shamelessly determined to fortify the validity of his deception, Jacob said the Lord had brought it to him. When Isaac requested that Jacob come near to him, Jacob's stomach must have twisted into knots as he approached his father. Isaac felt the back of Jacob's hand, which was covered in goatskin.

"The voice is Jacob's," Isaac reasoned in his bewilderment, "but the hands are Esau's." He asked again, "Are you my very son, Esau?"

"I am."

The rich aroma of the savory meat and broth permeated Isaac's nostrils. "Then bring my venison to me so that I may eat it and give you my blessing."

When he had finished eating, Isaac had an additional request. "Come near and kiss me, my son." Jacob undoubtedly took a deep breath as he gathered his frail father into his arms. Isaac smelled his clothes and discerned it was the scent of Esau. The smell reminded Isaac of the earthy richness of the soil; of a field blessed by God.

Satisfied, Isaac proclaimed, "Therefore, may God grant you gentle showers from heaven and the fertile soils of the earth, and rich harvests of grain and wine. May many peoples come and serve you, and may nations bow down to you. May you be the master of your brothers, and may your mother's sons all bow down before you. May anyone who curses you be cursed, and may everyone who blesses you be blessed!"

Incredible! Rebekah was right. The blessing Isaac had reserved for Esau was supreme, and now it belonged to Jacob. Jacob politely excused himself, likely to share the account of his newly received blessing with his mother. Shortly after Jacob left, Esau arrived with the venison he had prepared for his father and then echoed the words his brother had spoken earlier: "Please come, sit and eat of my venison. Then bless me as you have promised."

Isaac firmly demanded, "Who are you?"

Esau replied, "I am Esau, your firstborn!"

At that, Isaac began to shake violently. Suddenly, he realized he'd been tricked. "Who?" he cried. "Where is he that already served me venison that I ate and then blessed him?"

Surely, the memory of his lost birthright resounded in Esau's mind. He knew whatever blessing his lying brother had received was irrevocable and non-transferable to him. Fury like a fire smoldered within him as his anger was kindled. Hate began to roar throughout his soul. Weeping tears of bitterness, Esau cried helplessly, "Bless me, even me also, my father."

His father's words further assaulted him. "Your brother deceived me," Isaac said, "and has stolen your blessing."

"Is he not rightly named Jacob?" Esau spat the words. "He has supplanted me these two times, first with my birthright and now with my blessing." Then he asked in despondency, "Have you reserved a blessing for me?"

"I have made him your lord, and all his brothers have been given to him for servants. I have sustained him with corn and wine," Isaac conceded, knowing the blessing he had reserved for his firstborn son was forever forfeited from Esau. "What shall I do now to you, my son?" Isaac then blessed his son, but it hardly resembled what was originally reserved for him. "You will make your home far from the richness of the earth, far away from the gentle showers of heaven above. You will live by your sword, and you will serve your brother. But when you grow restless to be free, you will break his yoke from your neck."

From that day forward, Esau harbored a hateful grudge against Jacob and determined in his heart to kill him after his father died. When Rebekah realized this, she summoned Jacob, told him what Esau had planned, and arranged to send Jacob away to her brother's house. "Let's give your brother a few days to cool off from his anger." she reasoned. "Once he forgets what you did to him, I will send for you to come home again."[2]

Those "few days" turned into over twenty years, and apparently Rebekah never again saw her favored son before her death.

Isaac, finally realizing the divine destiny on Jacob's life, commended another blessing on his son before his departure. "May the All-Powerful God bless you, make you fruitful, and multiply your descendants so that you will give rise to nation after nation! May God give to you and to your children in this inheritance all of the blessings of Abraham, so that you might someday possess the land where you now live as a foreigner—a land that was promised by God to Abraham." Isaac's words resembled a covenant blessing originally given by *El Shaddai* to Abraham and now passed on to Jacob. (*El Shaddai* means "Almighty God" and defines him as the one who supports, defends, blesses, takes care of and supplies every need of his children.)[3]

Jacob regretfully said his goodbyes and then began his journey toward Haran, the home of his mother's brother, Laban. Remember, Jacob was more of a stay-at-home domestic momma's boy than the adventurous outdoor hunting type. Alone and with a heart filled with uncertainty, the remembrance of his father's blessings began fading. He was overwhelmed with the fear of the unknown compounded by his brother's hatred and plot to kill him. As Jacob traveled and meditated on these things, he must have prayed and called out to the Lord. Genesis later informs us that God answered him in his day of distress. About four days into the long journey, Jacob chose to settle as nightfall approached. He gathered some stones and made a pillow from them. Looking up into the star-filled heavens, he fell asleep.

As Jacob slumbered, God appeared to him in a dream and said, "I am the Lord God of Abraham your father and the God of Isaac; the land on which you lie I will give to you and your descendants. Also your descendants shall be as the dust of the earth; you shall spread abroad to the west and the east, to the north and the south; and in you and in your seed all the families of the earth shall be blessed. Behold, I am with you and will keep you wherever you go, and will bring you back to this land; for I will not leave you until I have done what I have spoken to you."

Alone and with a heart filled with uncertainty, the remembrance of his father's blessings began fading.

God responded to Jacob's time of stress with covenant promises like those he had made to Abraham, and by pledging that he would be with him like he swore to Isaac. God also gave Jacob his personal assurance to protect him, bring him into his destiny, and not leave until all was fulfilled. God's visit was not a result of Jacob's circumstances; he was calling Jacob into a relationship with him.

When Jacob woke up, he was full of awe and reverence from the visitation of the Lord God. Jacob poured oil on the stone he slept upon as a consecration to memorialize it as a holy place. He expressed honor for the Lord by naming the place "Bethel" meaning, *house of God*. Jacob also responded with these promises: "If God will help and protect me on this journey and give me food and clothes, and will bring me back safely to my father, then I will choose Jehovah as my God! And this memorial pillar shall become a place for worship; and I will give you back a tenth of everything you give me!"

Jehovah is a name that defines the Creator in relationship to that which he has created. This passage also indicates that Jacob tasted the goodness of Jehovah and was now seeking a living relationship with him rather than settling for some abstract acquaintance. Jacob had been upgraded from a conceptual knowledge about God to a genuine heartfelt experience with the living Lord—*El Shaddai*. This encounter laid the foundation of what would become Jacob's *God Place*.

Jacob arrived safely in Haran and met Laban and his daughters Leah and Rachel. Jacob fell in love with Rachel, the younger of the two sisters, and told Laban that he was willing to serve seven years to gain her hand in marriage. After the seven years, though, Laban tricked Jacob by delivering to him the older daughter, Leah, in the dark of the night, instead of Rachel. The next morning when it was daylight, Jacob was shocked to see that Leah was with him instead of Rachel. Jacob confronted Laban, who explained it was their custom to give the oldest daughter away first. Laban then offered Rachel, providing Jacob served an additional seven years. Throughout these years twelve sons were born between his two wives and their handmaidens. When his time of servitude was fulfilled, Jacob asked to leave with his wives and children, a share of the flocks he had tended for Laban and to return to his family. It was more than a reasonable request considering that during all of those years Laban had changed Jacob's wages and repeatedly taken advantage of him. Because of this, God blessed the flocks of Jacob while Laban's flocks did not flourish. Laban's displeasure seethed toward Jacob because of this request. An angel of the Lord told Jacob to flee and Jacob departed immediately with his family, livestock and possessions. It was three days before Laban figured out that Jacob had left. He pursued Jacob and his band and almost overtook them when God intervened, warning Laban in a dream not to speak either good or bad to Jacob.

The dream apparently upset Laban, because when he finally caught up to Jacob he exclaimed, "Why did you slip away secretly?

Why did you deceive me? And why didn't you say you wanted to leave? I would have given you a farewell feast, with singing and music, accompanied by tambourines and harps. Why didn't you let me kiss my daughters and grandchildren and tell them good-bye? You have acted very foolishly! I could destroy you, but the God of your father appeared to me last night and warned me, 'Leave Jacob alone!'" Jacob admitted that he fled without notice because he was afraid Laban was going to use force to keep his daughters at home. Then, Jacob angrily rebuked Laban, exclaiming, "What? Am I a criminal that you would hunt me down? What have I done to cause your pursuit? If God wasn't with me you would have sent me away empty-handed. But God saw the stress you were causing in my life and that is why he has warned you not to speak or act wrongly to me."[4]

Laban and Jacob decided to make an oath with each other, and with God as their witness, not to harm one another. Jacob additionally honored Laban's demand not to abuse his daughters or marry other wives.

After departing from Laban, Jacob decided to attempt to reconcile with Esau. Perhaps he hoped Esau's hatred and revengeful spirit had diminished over the past twenty years. Jacob sent messengers to Esau and asked to find favor in his sight. The messengers returned with the sobering news that Esau was on his way, with four hundred men to boot. How did Jacob take the news? "So Jacob was greatly afraid and distressed; and he divided the people that were with him, and the flocks and herds and camels, into two companies."

Despite the previous promises and multiple divine interventions, Jacob focused on the report and became terrified and stressed out about the "what ifs." Jacob divided the people and animals into two groups so if Esau attacked, only half would be lost and the other half could escape. Wisely, Jacob also went to his *God Place* and sought help from the Lord. He prayed, "God of my grandfather Abraham and God of my father Isaac! Lord, you said to me, 'Go back to your land and to your relatives, and I will make you prosperous.' I'm not worthy of all the love and faithfulness you have shown me. I only had a shepherd's staff when I crossed the Jordan River, but now I have two camps. Please save me from my brother Esau, because I'm afraid of him. I'm afraid that he'll come and attack me and my family, too. But you did say, 'I will make sure that you are prosperous and that your descendants will be as many as the grains of sand on the seashore. No one will be able to count them because there are so many.'"[5] Notice how Jacob was beginning to grow in his personal relationship with God: Jacob's prayer reiterated some of the promises that God had made to him earlier, and Jacob was also quite honest with the Lord as he admitted he was afraid while crying out for help.

The rest of this account (in Genesis 32) describes how Jacob set up three waves of blessings and gifts and sent his servants sequentially to Esau with the hope of appeasing him. When Esau and Jacob were within range of each other, Esau ran to meet Jacob, embraced him, and fell on his neck and kissed him. What a reunion that must have been! They exchanged respect, honor, forgiveness and mercy to one another as they wept in each other's arms.

In the end, they departed in peace. At that instant, Jacob realized that God had also touched Esau's heart and delivered him in his day of distress.

LESSONS LEARNED

This story of Jacob teaches us several lessons. First, when God makes a promise, he will faithfully fulfill it. The Book of Numbers reminds us, "God is not like people, who lie; He is not a human who changes his mind. Whatever he promises, he does; He speaks, and it is done."[6] He does not need our counsel, plans, or intervention to bring his promises to pass. God is the initiator of his will and we respond and partner to his revelation accordingly.

Sometimes, though, we can get this backwards and initiate our will, then ask God to bless it. How many things do we attribute to the Lord that are actually of our own doing? A good test of this question is realizing that God will never bless one person at the expense of being detrimental to others. The Bible informs us that God is not a respecter of persons. This means he does not discriminate or employ favoritism.[7] His invitation stands, beckoning "whoever" to come to him and experience his grace, truth, peace and love.

It's not surprising that even momentary departures from God's plan creates stress. Notice how easily stress starts out affecting an individual and then infiltrates the lives of those surrounding the individual and the situation. Stress came knocking when Jacob ruthlessly negotiated for Esau's birthright. Stress further moved into the lives of Isaac and Rebekah when Esau took Canaanite wives. Because Rebekah favored Jacob, she took providence into her own hands by scheming for a blessing reserved for Isaac's firstborn. As the combination of lies, deceit, envy and even the intent to commit murder gained influence, stress gripped the family and had its way with each member.

As Jacob habitually went to the *God Place* and called out to him for help, he began to know the Lord intimately. God was faithful to hear Jacob's plea and rescue him from his distress. Sometimes our prayers are similar to sending up a "distress signal." Like Jacob, when we encounter stress, we should seek our *God Place* and remind the Lord of the promises he has made. It's not because he needs the refresher—we do! Plus, it takes the focus off of our circumstances and places it on the greatness of God while reaffirming his faithfulness to our hearts and souls. It also increases our faith and decreases our stress. We don't bow to the problem, but to the one who provides the solution.

> *God will never bless one person at the expense of being detrimental to others.*

We don't bow to the problem, but to the one who provides the solution.

Here is another essential lesson. When we pray, it is best to be fully authentic and transparent with God. It does not reflect a lack of faith to tell God we are scared, sad, lonely or upset. He already knows all about it anyway. As we pray honestly, God will hear and answer our supplication. While we pour out our hearts to him, we also speak of his faithfulness with reassurance. God promises to bring us into an enlarged place as his deliverance relieves our stress and lifts our burdens.

Finally, employing ungodly practices rarely yields beneficial results in the long run. God by his grace and mercy has given us freedom of will. Even when we make foolish mistakes and overstep the divine design of submission to him, he provides a path of forgiveness. God's loyalty and love are as high as the heavens are above the earth. He removes our sins as far as the east is from the west.[8] (This description is notable, since north and south, geographically speaking, end at their respective poles. East and west, however, never meet because they have no end.) God knows of our human frailties and guides us back to the right way of his primary plan for our lives while helping us untangle our negative and stressful situations.

In the next chapter, we will look at the life of another Old Testament figure, David, and discover that stress sometimes comes our way even when we don't do anything to invite it.

References

1. Genesis 25:23 (CJB); Genesis 25:31b (ESV); Genesis 25:32 (VOICE) and Genesis 26:35 (NET)

2. Taken from: Genesis 27:2-4; Genesis 27:8-10; Genesis 27:13; Genesis 27:14-27; Genesis 27: 28 and 29 (VOICE); Genesis 27:30-33; Genesis 27:34-38; Genesis 27:39-40 (VOICE) and Genesis 27:41-45

3. Genesis 28:3-4 (VOICE); Genesis 28:13b-15 and Genesis 28:20b-22 (TLB)

4. Genesis 31:27-29 (NLT) and taken from Genesis 31:36-42

5. Genesis 32:7 and Genesis 32:9-12

6. Numbers 23:19 (GNT)

7. From 2 Chronicles 19:7

8. From Psalm 103:11 and 12

CHAPTER 5

HOW DAVID WAS RESCUED FROM STRESS

David's life was filled with good days and also not-so-good days. He was a shepherd, warrior, musician, poet, prophet, leader, politician and king. The greatest title bestowed upon him, though, was "a man after God's own heart."[1] Throughout the Scriptures, we are given the privilege of peeking into and even probing this heart of David's. When we peruse the Psalms, the expressions of David come to life and cause us to wonder how he endured his times of stress.

Saul, the first king of Israel, disobeyed and rejected God's counsel numerous times. This resulted in God rejecting Saul's leadership, and the throne was reserved for a young shepherd boy, a son of Jesse the Bethlehemite. God sent the prophet Samuel to Bethlehem where he was to anoint one of Jesse's son as the future king over Israel. When Samuel arrived, he took one look at Eliab, Jesse's eldest, and said to himself, "This must be the one." "But the Lord said to Samuel, 'Do not look at his appearance or at the height of his stature, because I have rejected him. For the Lord sees not as man sees; for man looks at the outward appearance, but the Lord looks at the heart.'"[2] After seven of Jesse's sons passed before Samuel, he discerned that none of them were the chosen king. Samuel asked whether there were any other sons. Jesse reluctantly admitted his youngest, David, was out tending to the sheep. Samuel requested Jesse to summon him. When he was brought before Samuel, God revealed that David was the one.

That very day Samuel anointed David with oil and the Spirit of God came upon the son who was the least likely candidate. This Spirit is what enabled David to have relational connection with God.

Later that year, David became famous with his slaying of the Philistine giant, Goliath. David's popularity grew with the people as they sang and danced, "Saul hath slain his thousands, and David his ten thousands."[3] The Philistines soon became familiar with this song as well. These celebrations of David's victories caused Saul to seethe with jealousy. As he became afraid of David's sterling reputation within the kingdom, Saul's fear provoked his resolve to end the young hero's life. Saul's son, Jonathan, became an intimate friend of David's, and temporarily convinced his father to allow David to live. Saul nevertheless was capricious, and from time to time his murderous fury was rekindled forcing David to flee and hide.

As the stability of the Saul's kingdom waned, many people grew dissatisfied and sought alternative leadership. David's successful influence attracted his brethren, members of his household, and others embittered with Saul. When they heard of David's whereabouts, they sought him for leadership and resources. It is written of David, "And every one in distress, and every one that was in debt, and every one of embittered spirit collected round him; and he became a captain over them; and there were with him about four hundred men."[4] As David trained his troops, their loyalty was nurtured. When Saul learned of David's faithful brigade, his determination to kill David and all who were with him intensified. In these times of incredible distress, David grew in his ability to rely on his relationship with God. He yearned to commune with him in the *God Place*, where he received answers, wisdom and direction.

1 Samuel 24 tells us that one day David was hiding out in a cave with his men. Saul, who had learned of David's whereabouts, pursued him into the wilderness of Engedi. Entering a cave, Saul postured to relieve himself. Ironically, it was the very cave where David and his

men were concealed. It was almost laughable. "Look!" one of David's men whispered to him. "God has delivered the enemy into your hand." David snuck up on Saul and quietly cut a piece of cloth from his outfit, but chose not to assault or kill him. Then we learn David's heart convicted him for even doing that feeble act, because David understood Saul was anointed of the Lord. David sharply persuaded his overanxious men to refrain from attacking Saul, and the king went on his way without realizing he had almost been assassinated. That is, until David called out to Saul from the mouth of the cave and told him that while David's men had begged him to kill Saul, he had chosen to save his life. As proof, David humbly waved the piece of cloth he had cut from Saul's robe.

David explained that his heart was convicted as he suddenly recalled Saul was anointed of the Lord. David, therefore, promised God not to harm him. As Saul regained his composure, he recognized that David had dealt well with him. Saul lauded David for his kindness and admitted that the Lord had indeed given him the throne of Israel. Saul then had David swear to not wipe out Saul's family after he became king or destroy Saul's namesake. David agreed and Saul returned home, while David and his men remained in the wilderness.

Saul's commitment to peace with David, however, was short lived. Once again the king began to aggressively hunt down David and his men. As recorded in 1 Samuel 26, David had yet another opportunity to kill Saul. But David acknowledged Saul's anointing and that his life was in God's hands alone. Saul again admitted his error, repented and promised to no longer pursue David.

Unconvinced of Saul's integrity, David went to the Philistine city of Gath. There he requested of King Achish a place in the country where he and his men could dwell in safety away from Saul. Achish gave David and his men their own city called Ziklag, and for the next sixteen months they helped Achish fight battles against his enemies. When the Philistine princes heard about this, though, they approached the king with great concern and reminded him that David could turn on him at any time.

While Achish trusted David with his life, he felt it best for David and his men to return to Ziklag and not to continue fighting in the Philistine battles, especially when it was against the Israelites. Disdained, David informed his loyal company that they were no longer needed as an army, and as the new dawn arose, they set out on their journey back to Ziklag. The men marched about seventeen miles a day, from sunrise to sundown for three days, longing to see their families and enjoy the comforts of home.[5]

As they approached Ziklag, smoke drifted into the air from afar. The faint smell of the fire reminded them of home-cooked meals and warm family gatherings. Climbing over the last hill, Ziklag was finally in view, but what they saw was shocking. The Amalekites had invaded Ziklag from the south, and then burned it with fire. In terror, David's soldiers broke rank and ran toward their city and smoldering houses. Frantically searching up and down the rubble-strewn streets, they eventually realized with a gut-wrenching dismay that their wives and children had been taken captive and their homes plundered. David and his men cried out loudly and wept, until they had no more power to weep. That's when grief abruptly turned to rage as David's loyal men, the very men he had trained and taken care of, turned on him in bitter blame and forged a plot to put him to death. The Bible says, "And David was greatly distressed, for the people spoke of stoning him because the soul of all the people was grieved, every man for his sons and for his daughters; but David encouraged himself in the Lord his God."[6]

David's stress had reached unfathomable proportions. He wept with uncontrollable emotion, and his mind raced with sorrowful regret. Rejection saturated every fiber of his being as he reflected on the events of his life, and how his family had never considered him more than a "ruddy youth." Or how Saul, full of envy, had chased after him to murder him. Or how the people of Keilah, a city in Judah, had sided with Saul's rejection of him and conspired to turn him in. Then even the Philistine king, Achish, the enemy of Israel, had informed David that he was no longer needed. Now David faced the loss of the loyalty of his men, his family, his property and possibly his life. With unyielding problems assailing his senses, maybe he considered, *Will God now turn his back on me as well?* Many times, circumstances shake up our surroundings and reveal the instability and condition of our hearts.

Many times, circumstances shake up our surroundings and reveal the instability and condition of our hearts.

THE TURNING POINT

David's story is not unique: even while writing this chapter, I encountered a series of debilitating, back-to-back challenges. Only one month earlier, life had been teeming with opportunities for ministry, prosperity, vision and vibrant fellowship with others. I felt like I was cruising life's highway at eighty miles per hour with the top down and the wind racing through my hair. Then, it all suddenly seemed to come to a screeching halt. Friends who I trusted had broken promises, and I encountered the compromised integrity of other associates. Even the expected replies from correspondence were never returned. My invested passions, resources, and finances had failed to produce the anticipated results. Contributions to our ministry diminished, and disappointments, deceit, slander and rejection came crashing in like unstoppable waves. Loneliness gripped my soul like the silent chill of a dark, cold winter's night. "What is going on?" I cried out to God. While my experience was surely nowhere near David's level of stress, I realized the answer lied in doing the same thing David did.

Look again at his response to catastrophe. It was both glorious and astonishing:

"But David encouraged himself in the LORD his God."

"But" is a conjunction which contrasts that which proceeds with that which follows. Instead of remaining greatly stressed, David encouraged himself in the Lord. He was determined to go to his *God Place* at the time of his life-draining distress. This word "encouraged" is intriguing. In other Bible verses it is rendered as *strengthened, fortified, secured, sustained, retained or prevailed upon.* While the Scriptures do not detail how David encouraged himself in the Lord, they reveal many aspects of his heart for God. A passage from 1 Samuel informs us, "Then Jonathan, Saul's son, arose and went to David in the woods and strengthened his hand in God. And he said to him, 'Do not fear, for the hand of Saul my father shall not find you. You shall be king over Israel, and I shall be next to you. Even my father Saul knows that.'"[7]

In this record, "strengthened" is the same Hebrew word as "encouraged" in the previous verse, "But David *encouraged* himself in the LORD his God." Sometimes we need a true friend to share about their experiences in the *God Place*, someone to help strengthen and encourage us in the Lord. Jonathan reiterated and confirmed a prophecy previously spoken over David, bringing David refreshment and restoration. I am reminded of two Proverbs:

"A man has joy in giving an appropriate answer, And how good and delightful is a word spoken at the right moment—how good it is!"

"Like apples of gold in settings of silver, Is a word spoken in right circumstances."

In the biblical times when Proverbs was written, apples had not yet been cultivated. However, there is a kind of orange, called *kitchilika* in Sanskrit, that was fragrant and the size of a grapefruit. Its fresh juice was typically served in silver pitchers on silver trays and especially appreciated by weary travelers on hot days. This invigorating beverage had the quality of rejuvenating and strengthening both the body and soul. Words from God spoken in love to someone at just the right time bring encouragement, revitalization and renewal to both the speaker and the recipient.[8]

Even as a young boy, David had a relationship with the Lord. His great grandmother Ruth, known as a remarkable and virtuous woman, played an integral part in providing a vital foundation and reverence for God. Perhaps he played his harp and sang songs to the Lord while in the meadow watching over the sheep. David was also schooled in the Torah (the first five books of the Hebrew Scriptures) and therefore learned about Moses. Maybe he recalled the many times Moses called out to God for help. Certainly remembrance of Scripture brought back truths about the faithfulness of his Lord. David was intimate with God as a young man, building his trust in the Lord. He wrote in Psalm 18, "I love you, O Lord, my strength. The Lord is my rock and my fortress and my deliverer, my God, my rock, in whom I take refuge, my shield, and the horn of my salvation, my stronghold."[9] Notice the many times "my" is used in the passage. Replace each "my" with *your* name. Boldly speak each declaration aloud. Receive them as your very own promises from the Lord your God, and reflect on each one as an evident part of your mutual relationship with him. We can't say we are his until we say he is ours!

As David cultivated his *God Place*, deepening his relationship with the Lord over the years, he learned to be patient and wait on him. David penned, "Wait on the Lord: be of good courage, and he shall strengthen thine heart: wait, I say, on the Lord.[10] What does it mean to wait on God? I hear people say, "Well, I'm just waiting on the Lord." Most of the time that's an excuse, explaining why their prayers are not being answered in a timely fashion. The perception of God taking forever to help is a misconception. Here is a better insight: "Behold, as the eyes of servants look to the hand of their master, as the eyes of a maidservant to the hand of her mistress, so our eyes look to the Lord our God, till he has mercy upon us."[11]

In the culture and times of David, servants were trained to be attentive to their master's every move. They focused on the master, anticipating either a request or a command. If you have ever experienced dining in a restaurant where professionally trained servers are seen standing off in the distance yet watching over your table, and who gracefully approach to refill water glasses, replenish the bread basket, or clear away the plates, then you have an idea of what waiting on God means. It is a vivid and instructive word picture. The Hebrew word for wait portrays a picture of strands of threads (usually plant fibers or animal hair) being braided together to form a rope. It represents strength and unity. When we focus on God and intertwine our hearts with his, we line up our will with his will and experience his strength and purposes.

When we focus on God and intertwine our hearts with his, we line up our will with his will and experience his strength and purposes.

Proverbs emphatically instructs, "Above all else, guard your heart, for everything you do flows from it."[12] A constant fellowship with God fosters partnership with him, and as we encourage our hearts in him, he strengthens our hearts while we look to him and wait for his advice. If we don't like what is happening in our lives, then we need to guard our hearts by confronting, examining and correcting our thoughts and actions. What are we putting into our minds and hearts? Does it draw us closer to God or subtly influence us to drift from him?

A book called The Song of Solomon conveys another concept regarding guarding our hearts, only it uses an illustration from agricultural practices. "The little foxes are ruining the vineyards.

Catch them, for the grapes are all in blossom."¹³ Vineyards were surrounded by hedges to keep intruders out and to mark boundaries. When the grapes were young and tender a watchman was hired to protect the fruit. Little foxes tried to get through the hedge and if they succeeded, they not only ate the grapes, but dug up the root of the vines, destroying them also. In this analogy, the vineyard is the heart. The hedge is the mind, acting as a barrier of protection around what enters the heart. The tender grapes represent newly introduced promises of God's goodness. The little foxes (small thoughts) try to break through the hedge around the heart to destroy one's confidence in God's encouraging thoughts. We are the watchmen guarding our minds and hearts from negative thinking. We don't want stressful thoughts of doubt, defeat, destruction or doom infiltrating our minds and rooting up the fruitful promises of God. God wants us to think positively. Our hearts should be flourishing with thoughts of blessed days, success, abundance and peace. Have you heard of the expression, "entertaining a thought?" Suppose a negative thought knocked at your front door, would you invite it in and say, "Please, make yourself at home. How about a cup of tea?" Of course not! You would cautiously peer through the door and ask, "Who is it?"

The apostle Paul wrote in the letter to the Philippians; "In conclusion, my friends, fill your minds with those things that are good and that deserve praise: things that are true, noble, right, pure, lovely, and honorable."¹⁴

Thinking that the worst possible event might happen lets the little foxes in. Entering into negative discussions only makes a wider gap in the hedge. Extreme negativity such as, "It *always* happens to me" or "*Nobody* likes me" is destructive to the heart. We dare not entertain what we perceive others are thinking about us. When we take our hearts to God and put them in the palm of his hands, we will count our blessings and reinforce the hedge.

It is important for us to understand that *relationship* with God, not technique, is the foundation for deliverance from every stress we encounter. It's easy to fall into formulaic practices, trying to please God in order to get a response from him. This includes feeling the need to do more of some "religious" activity, or us attempting to make something happen in order to succeed. It is through our relationship with him that we find the best counsel and direction on *how* to proceed. God's help may, but frequently may not include our self-governed intentions.

Our relationship with the Lord is the essence of the *God Place*. Sometimes God told David to pursue and fight the enemy. Other times he instructed David to rest in him and be still. How did David know? He kept his focus on the Lord, waiting for his instruction, and by not dwelling on the problems perceived by his five senses. As we continue to go to the *God Place*, he will teach us and help us grow in our relationship with him in the same way he did with David. Part of that growth may involve degrees of praying, praising, meditating on and confessing God's promises, and fellowshipping with spiritually mature friends. As we practice being quiet and listening while waiting on God for an answer, our hearts will be woven into the tapestry of his living presence. These are just some of the things that David, the man after God's own heart, nurtured in his daily and ongoing fellowship with the Lord. We can learn so much about the *God Place* by examining David's relationship with God as it is recorded in the Scriptures.

> *It is important for us to understand that relationship with God, not technique, is the foundation for deliverance from every stress we encounter.*

Even as I continue writing this chapter, it is humbling to discover the increasing need to become immersed in the *God Place*. I desire to proclaim like David: "I long to drink of you, O God, drinking deeply from the streams of pleasure flowing from your presence. My longings overwhelm me for more of you!"[15] It is vital for me to draw nearer to God because anytime stress intensifies its grasp on me, so does the temptation to yield to other suggestions rather than reaching out directly to him for help. As Proverbs warns, "If you fail under pressure, your strength is too small."[16] Focusing on problems instead of God's solutions tends to make our issues too big and our God too small. Our strength is not only *in* him—it *is* him! As I too confront crippling challenges in the same way David did, I am encouraging myself in the Lord my God! I won't let go of him until he reveals what is going on and what to do about it.

> *Focusing on problems instead of God's solutions tends to make our issues too big and our God too small.*

It has been a while since that stressful time of my life came upon me. I relentlessly sought God and he, as promised, delivered me from my distress. Specifically, I was reminded of the spiritual battle against the devil and his kingdom of darkness. The weapons used to engage in this warfare are not worldly, but powered by God. Circumstances may try to bombard the mind, but God is mightier that any opposition. Relying on him is the key to victorious living. So God, through his infinite grace, love and wisdom, restored that which was taken and brought new and better resources into my life. Not content with that, he continues to teach me deeper truths as I pursue him in the *God Place*.

ACT ON GOD'S DIRECTION

David neither bowed to his circumstances nor did he blame God or even the people who wanted to kill him. He didn't sink into a pity party or wallow in guilt and condemnation. Instead, he diligently went after God, communed with him, and consulted him for the right direction and best remedy for his dilemma.

"So David inquired of the Lord, saying, 'Shall I pursue this troop? Shall I overtake them?' And He answered him, 'Pursue, for you shall surely overtake them and without fail recover all.'"[17]

David not only heard the voice of the Lord, he *obeyed* the voice of God because of the promise. It was David's obedience that delivered him from stress and caused a victorious outcome. Obedience to God continues to be a remarkably misunderstood subject often offending the rebellious heart.

I am aware of two types of obedience. One involves a joyful submission and response because it is rooted in a loving relationship with a bonding trust between two or more individuals. The other represents a half-hearted act of obligation with a veneer of compliance. Beneath the surface hides the fear of consequences from disobedience. Additionally, in this second kind of obedience, the relationship between these two or more individuals lacks trust.

Trust draws its breath from honesty and truth which constitute God's infinitely virtuous character. What is the motive of our hearts? Does our obedience to God flow from love or obligation? Our response will be influenced by our level of trust in him. This sheds light on why God looks at the heart. Trust is incubated in the *God Place* and blossoms through a budding relationship with him. Like any relationship, it takes time.

Once we seek God's help and he shows us what to do, our response is to *act* on God's revelation, and then we will see his promises prevail. "So David recovered all that the Amalekites had carried away, and David rescued his two wives. And nothing of theirs was lacking, either small or great, sons or daughters, spoil or anything which they had taken from them; David recovered all."[18] David and his men also took possession of all the treasures that the Amalekites had plundered from other enemies but left behind when they fled. At about the same time, Saul and Jonathan were both killed in battle, and David became king—just as Samuel the prophet had foretold.

David continued to be a man after God's own heart. Psalm 34 summarizes his life during the good days and the not so good ones: "I will bless the Lord at all times; His praise shall continually be in my mouth."[19] This is the language of the *God Place*.

I encourage you to read more about David's life from the Bible. You will be drawn into feeling the emotions of his heart and get a picture of how intimacy with God relieves the intensity of stress. The greater the stress, the greater the intimacy required for deliverance!

God promised to never leave or forsake David, and that promise is also for us. The inspirational lessons of David's journey offer wonderful perspectives on the *God Place*, illuminating the benefits of growing in an intimate relationship with the Lord.

Next, we will look at the life of one of David's associates, someone who had been close to God, but was pulled away by getting wrapped up in other matters rather than staying rooted in the things of God. Though you are not likely to recall his name, his story provides more insights on overcoming stress God's way.

References
1.   1 Samuel 13:14
2.   1 Samuel 16:7 (AMP)
3.   1 Samuel 18:7
4.   1 Samuel 22:2 (DBY)
5.   See 1 Samuel 27 and 29:3-11
6.   See 1 Samuel 30:1-6 (KJ21)
7.   1 Samuel 23:16-17
8.   Proverbs 15:23 (AMP); Proverbs 25:11 (NAS) and http://www.kcpillai.org/bishop-kc-pillai/ori-entalisms
9.   Psalm 18:1 and 2 (ESV)
10.   Psalm 27:14 (KJV)
11.   Psalm 123:2 (ESV)
12.   Proverbs 4:23 (NIV)
13.   Song of Solomon 2:15 (TLB)
14.   Philippians 4:18 (GNT)

The God Place

15. Psalm 42:1 (TPT)
16. Proverbs 24:10 (NLT)
17. 1 Samuel 30:8
18. 1 Samuel 30:18 and 19
19. Psalm 34:1

CHAPTER 6

HOW ASAPH WAS RESCUED FROM STRESS

Throughout history, many of the great men and women who God has called to be ministers and prophets have also been—musicians! Moses was a composer as was his sister Miriam. The book of Judges mentions Deborah's song of praise to God. In the days when Saul was king of Israel, there was a company of prophets with musical instruments. David played and sang praises before the Lord with all of his might, and David's son, Solomon, composed over one thousand songs. Praising God with music has always moved people's hearts closer to him. He delights to hear our voices ring with a joyful noise.

When David became king, he appointed a man named Asaph, a Levite and a prophet, to become one of his chief musicians. Asaph's job was to offer music before the Ark of the Covenant, which was located within the tabernacle. The Ark represented the presence of God. Asaph had the daily responsibility of leading the praise and worship of the congregation before the Lord. Under King David's leadership Asaph's ministry brought a renewal of desire for the things of God and a rekindled hunger for the Lord's presence. Asaph was instrumental in helping people discover the *God Place*.

Imagine the excitement of this passionate celebration! Oh how people's souls must have been lifted up in joyous expression, inundated by the majestic sound of instruments and voices—and the sight of worshipful dance. Asaph must have thrown all of his physical and emotional abilities into each service.

Yet sometimes the thrill of praise and worship can be subtly mistaken as constituting a personal, intimate relationship with God. Our relationship with God cannot be substituted by or couched behind the outward appearances of praise and worship. True praise and worship is a response; it ripens as our relationship with him deepens.

One great lesson we learned from observing David's life was that he looked to God and God alone. Genuine praise and worship is a declaration of who God is; it is not about us (including how we feel). Asaph wrote twelve Psalms by the inspiration of God. Yet in the routine of his daily duties as a music minister, Asaph allowed his eyes to gradually wander from the Lord as he became consumed with himself and others. As we shall see, the *ritual* of praise and worship could never replace Asaph's eroding relationship with the Lord, which became a source of stress in Asaph's life. Let's look at two of his psalms to discover more lessons on being rescued from stress.

PSALM 73: REPENT AND REFOCUS

Psalm 73 opens with praise. "Surely God is good to Israel, to those who are pure in heart." But by the second verse, Asaph's story begins to fluctuate as he alleges, "But as for me, my feet had almost slipped; I had nearly lost my foothold."

Asaph quickly deviated to a "me, myself, and I syndrome." He continued, "For I envied the arrogant when I saw their wicked prosperity." And then he began comparing his life to theirs. "Indulging in whatever they wanted, going where they wanted, doing what they wanted, and with no care in the world. No pain, no problems, they seemed to have it made. They lived as though life would never end." Asaph introduced stress into his life as he inadvertently allowed the dynamics of his focus to shift from God onto himself. Even though he went into the sanctuary daily, a representation of the *God Place*, he permitted his heart to stray from the presence of the Lord. This can happen to any of us no matter how rooted we may think we are in the things of God. Once that occurs, our perception may curtail to a distorted view of who God is and also who we are in relation to him and those around us.

Deteriorated thinking and increased muttering led Asaph further away from the truth and slowly enticed him toward the path of deception. "They wear pride like a jeweled necklace and clothe themselves with cruelty. These fat cats have everything their hearts could ever wish for! They scoff and speak only evil; in their pride they seek to crush others. They boast against the very heavens, and their words strut throughout the earth. And so the people are dismayed and confused, drinking in all their words. 'What does God know?' they ask. 'Does the Most High even know what's happening?'"

Asaph's heart grew unthankful. He began to actually believe that God was doing him an injustice. The more he rehearsed his opinions, the more convinced he became that they were true. His distraction intensified even more as he continued to agonize and compare himself with others. *Have I been foolish to play by the rules and keep my life pure?* Remember that Asaph began this Psalm by proclaiming God is good to those pure in heart. Now he professed that God was treating unbelievers better than his own people. Asaph bought into the lie that unbelievers were prospering, that they had no problems, essentially living stress-free lives. He felt God was not faithful, and reasoned, *Why bother?* He thought it was useless for him to cleanse his ways and walk with the Lord. Like loose trash swirling about on a blustery day, regrets agitated his mind with tempestuous confusion. "My life is full of trouble and all I get is reproof and rebuke every morning," he lamented.

Asaph believed his begrudging experiences were the wages of serving God. This trap is easily entered by those who feel God is obligated to bless them, especially materially, for good deeds done in his name. You probably are familiar with those who try to play "Let's Make A Deal" with God by pitching the promise, "If you do this, then I will do that," or "Don't you see my activities done in your name? Now, where is my prize?" If we determine our relationship with God through self-righteous performances, we may demand or expect things from him that he never offered to begin with. This will put us on the road to Unhappyville. God's good gifts are promises and blessings which cannot be earned.

Now, seething in bitterness, Asaph moans. "If I'd have given in and talked like this, I would have betrayed your dear children. Still, when I tried to figure it out, all I got was a splitting headache." Asaph thought about all the service he did in the temple and wondered why God reserved his choicest blessings for the ungodly. Shrugging his shoulders and throwing up his hands, Asaph felt too frustrated to discuss this matter with anyone because he didn't want to appear as a bad influence. He was ready to give up everything he had been called to do and everything he believed in. Although he went through the daily rituals of praise and worship, his heart was far from either one. He just wanted to quietly slip out the back door after each service so that he wouldn't poison others with his hypocritical attitude. Trying to sort it all out seemed impossible and too painful. Asaph believed he couldn't open his heart to anyone.

His life had reached an incredibly low ebb. Even the slightest thought about his situation provoked his already stressed-out soul. It is important to recognize and learn the lesson from this account. Anyone, even the most well-intentioned servants of God, can stray from their *God Place*.

But as we soon discover in the next verses of this Psalm, the winds of change began to gently blow the fragrance of favor. No matter how deep we sink, the mighty hand of God is both willing and able to reach down and pull us out of the mire of despair and renew our child-like relationship with him.

Suddenly, Asaph experienced an "aha" moment: "Then I went into your sanctuary, O God, and I finally understood the destiny of the wicked." This sanctuary was not referring to the temple, the physical place where he went to work; rather, it indicated the presence of the living Lord, the *God Place*. Asaph wasn't going into the sanctuary, but into the arms of the one it represented. Asaph's attention started to shift back to seeking his true love, the Lord God. "Then I saw the whole picture: The slippery road you've put them on, with a final crash in a ditch of delusions. In the blink of an eye, disaster! A blind curve in the dark, and—nightmare! We wake up and rub our eyes....Nothing. There's nothing to them. And there never was."

Anyone, even the most well-intentioned servants of God, can stray from their God Place.

Only the Lord could have revealed these deep truths to Asaph as he communed with him in the true sanctuary of his heart, the *God Place*. These verses describe God allowing certain situations to occur due to the insistent freewill of humankind. Earlier, Asaph felt like he was slipping and that the unbelievers were the favored ones. God revealed to Asaph the reality and destiny of those very ones of whom Asaph was jealous. Eternal life with God was to be prized over temporal earthly existence, and this revelation of salvation both rescued and relieved Asaph from his relentless stress. Like the beacon from a lighthouse, God guided Asaph's back to the peaceful harbor of his intimate care for him. Asaph repented and sobbed. "Then I realized that my heart was bitter, and I was all torn up inside." As the Lord gave him understanding, Asaph's once passionate fire for God reignited from a faintly glowing ember to a roaring blaze.

Repentance is not feeling sorry for ourselves, apologizing, and then going about our merry way while not doing anything about what needs changing. Genuine repentance comes when we realize we are proceeding in the wrong direction and then choosing to change, turn around and move in the right direction. Asaph continued, "I was stupid and ignorant. I was like a beast before you! Nevertheless, I am continually with you: you hold me by my right hand. You will guide me with your counsel, and afterward receive me to glory." As he confessed his sin, Asaph realized how self-consumed he had become. A beast is like a wild animal that reacts to what it perceives. Asaph's lost his identity due to his preconceived, self-propagated ideas. Yet throughout his calamity, God was holding his right hand, the hand of blessing. God also promised to guide Asaph and receive him into glory. What a revelation! Asaph began to understand how stress during one's limited days on earth pales when compared to the magnificent glory of eternal life.

Now Asaph's self-absorption and vocabulary shifted from "me, myself, and I" back to God: right where it belonged the whole time. "You're all I want in heaven! You're all I want on earth! When my skin sags and my bones get brittle, God is rock-firm and faithful. Look! Those who left you are falling apart! Deserters, they'll never be heard from again. But I'm in the very presence of God—oh, how refreshing it is! I've made Lord God my home. God, I'm telling the world what you do!" Asaph came to the realization that everything wasn't all about him. It was all about the one who created him. Despite his weaknesses and shortcomings, God was faithful and loving to Asaph. As the ones who Asaph envied were now brought to true light, what did he proclaim was good? To be in the very presence of God and in true relationship with him. This stirred up a genuine praise for God (vertically) which was then shared with overflowing joy (horizontally). My friends, this is the *God Place*![1]

There may be times when we feel we need to act as if we have it all together, yet in reality, our heart is far from the God. During those times, we tend to focus on ourselves and our perceived needs or injustices we have suffered. Self-focus pulls us away from God and his watchful care and direction over our lives. This self-centeredness increases our stress level, but we may be rescued from ourselves by God's wisdom. Then our stress will be alleviated as we turn our hearts back and decide to trust in the Lord once again.

PSALM 77: ASAPH'S EMOTIONS WHILE DEALING WITH HIS DAY OF DISTRESS

The Bible helps us identify with different characters and their emotions as they were rescued from stress. Asaph began Psalm 77 with a desperate heart crying out to the Lord at the top of his lungs. God heard and responded to Asaph's frantic appeal. Seeking God sometimes requires a voice of urgency. Our soul needs an articulate way to express its desperate cry for help. Asaph gives us an example of how to do this. After opening with an urgent cry he continues, "When I was in deep distress, in my day of trouble, I reached out for you with hands stretched out to heaven."

Seeking God is our responsibility. Responding to us is his responsibility, and God is faithful. Even though Asaph went so far as to stretch out his hands for help, his soul refused to be comforted as there seemed to be no remedy in sight. His stressful situation was persistent and agitating, and it relentlessly caused him to toss and turn through the night. Asaph's distracted mind obscured the reality of the presence of God, and the doubt in his heart refused any consoling help. The description of Asaph's soul is reminiscent of an exhausted and fussy baby that rebuffs all of its mother's pacifying care.

Asaph groaned, "I remembered God, and was troubled: I complained, and my spirit was overwhelmed. Selah." Even the slightest reflection upon God exacerbated Asaph's stress and caused him to protest. His spirit, referring to the spirit of humankind and commonly translated "soul," was devastated. As our soul becomes overwhelmed with stress, peace wanders far from us. Asaph's faith had eroded into unbelief, and God's promises seemed out of reach, causing even more frustration. Let's not rush past the last word in this verse, "Selah." It means to *pause, consider,* and *meditate* upon these words. The Bible is God-inspired, and Selah is used by him to emphasize the verses that precede the expression.

Asaph continued murmuring, "I cannot sleep until you act. I am too distressed even to pray."[2] His rest was robbed because his restless soul knew no peace and had no hope. There is a verse in Proverbs which explains: "When hope's dream seems to drag on and on, the delay can be depressing. But when at last your dream comes true, life's sweetness will satisfy your soul."[3] A stormy soul is an enemy of tranquility. Like a shipwrecked sailor tossed to and fro in a tempestuous ocean of doubt, Asaph could not navigate his way out of his circumstances or recognize God's outstretched hand of deliverance.

As Asaph searched his heart, he recounted the numerous testimonies recited to him about the wondrous God who delivered his ancestors in former times. Asaph's upbringing, instruction from the Torah and testimonies of God's goodness were rooted in the depths of his soul. He remembered songs sung to him as a child, praises of rejoicing accompanied by music and even songs he had composed for God. Asaph may have recalled one of those songs sung in the sanctuary or even a time when God sang an original heavenly melody to him. I am reminded of this passage. "For the LORD your God is living among you. He is a mighty savior. He will take delight in you with gladness. With His love, he will calm all your fears. He will rejoice over you with joyful songs."[4]

When we are reminded of God's faithful participation in our past predicaments, we will develop hope toward the future.

The Jewish day began at sunset. To begin their new day, the culture customarily embraced their evenings with devotion to God. This time of reflection imparted rest to them. Although Asaph attempted to do this, his mind still roamed and grew restless like a turbulent wave swelling back and forth.

Now Asaph moans, "Has the Lord rejected me forever? Will he never again be favorable? Is his loving-kindness gone forever? Has his promise failed? Has he forgotten to be kind to one so undeserving? Has he slammed the door in anger on his love?" In many translations of this passage, "Selah" is written once again after these exclamations so that the reader may pause and consider these words. Perhaps we've also harbored similar thoughts toward God on occasion.

Frazzled with frustration, Asaph surmised, *What hurts me most is this—that God is no longer powerful.*

Then suddenly, like a lifeguard discovering a drowning swimmer desperately thrashing and barely staying above the waves, God dashed after Asaph's heart and breathed life into his memory. As Asaph considered his past encounters with trouble, he recalled how God had been faithful to hear his cry and rescue him. His day of distress began to pivot toward his day of deliverance as he declared, "I will remember the deeds of the Lord; yes, I will remember your miracles of long ago."

"I will," was the victory cry of Asaph as he deliberately decided to center his thoughts on God's delivering power rather than accusing him of abandonment. When we are reminded of God's faithful participation in our past predicaments, we will develop hope toward the future. Like a pressure cooker release valve, our trust in God will relieve the simmering stress of our soul in the midst of our dilemma.

As Asaph returned his heart to God, his remembrance of the Lord's graciousness and faithfulness eclipsed his unthankful attitude and encouraged him to meditate upon God's greatness instead of his weakness. Meditation is a lost art! What is commonly called meditation today has its roots in mysticism and is convoluted with the integration of pagan rituals. As Asaph truly meditated on God (and not himself or others) he began to rehearse and confess the righteous works of God's goodness. Asaph concluded that God's ways were holy, there was no other god as awesome, and that through his amazing wonders, God demonstrated his strength by redeeming and delivering his people. Selah![5]

GOD'S CALMING WORDS

The Psalms written by Asaph, and really all of the Psalms, are poetic expressions of God's heart. Selah is one of the most beautiful words of the Psalms. *The Passion Translation* notes that Selah means to pause in the Lord's presence. It is an invitation to enter the *God Place*. Now is the time for you to pause, put your stressful and distracting problems on hold. Turn your heart away from stewing over those negative life-draining pressures and affectionately gaze upon the living God who has the solutions to all of your problems. There is no formula to follow, no technique to prescribe; it all comes down to cultivating a heart that seeks the Lord. Remember! God looks at the heart. As you pause in his presence, he will reveal himself to you and speak calming words of deliverance to your soul. Welcome to the *God Place*!

Psalm 107 illustrates different scenarios of life, yet each one reveals how consistently God intervenes whenever and wherever the "whoever" cries out to him. Verse 4 of Psalm 107 mentions those who are wandering with no direction, even to the point of thirst, starvation, and physical desperation. When their souls cried out to God in their day of distress, he heard them and led them to a safe place of abundance where they could settle. Perhaps you, too, lack direction and feel restless and physically distraught. Maybe you are spiritually hungering and thirsting for answers, direction, relief and provision. God will hear and respond to your cry for help. There is a wise saying from Proverbs that echoes the Psalmist: "Trust in *and* rely confidently on the Lord with all your heart And do not rely on your own insight *or* understanding. In all your ways know and acknowledge and recognize Him, And He will make your paths straight and smooth [removing obstacles that block your way]."[6]

God grants us joy in discovering his ways. He generously provides direction for all our decisions, big or small. But it is really up to us. Notice the three requirements we should employ: 1) Trust and rely confidently on him, which means totally depend on God with all, not half, of our hearts. 2) Don't rely on our own insights or understanding—our own abilities to figure everything out. 3) Acknowledge and recognize him in all our ways, again, totally and not half-heartedly. When we do our part, it invites God to fulfill his promise. He will make your paths straight and smooth, removing obstacles that block your way.

There is hidden treasure within this passage. When this Proverb was written, it was customary for dignitaries to visit various communities. As the people in the towns and villages heard that these distinguished guests were approaching, they sent out work crews ahead of time to prepare the way. This included removing rocks, fallen trees and other debris from the road. Next they graded the path, alleviating any ruts for the comfort of the travelers and allowing the downpour of rain to run off to the sides and not form puddles. This diligent gesture demonstrated love, honor and respect for their esteemed visitors. Now, the way into the community provided a well-marked, safe and welcoming entrance. Whenever we are expecting a visit from family, friends or guests, don't we want to prepare to graciously receive them? Think about God anticipating our arrival to commune with him. He directs us to a path that always leads us to the *God Place*. He sends out the work crews ahead of time to ensure our journey is smooth and that the directions are clear. We are treated as royalty, with love, honor and respect. There is a calming confidence found in God that will inspire you to apply his wisdom.

Psalm 107:10 presents those who rebelliously rejected God's

counsel and wisdom. Chained to their problems and ensnared by their past, they helplessly sink deeper in the quicksand of circumstances. Their hope of freedom dims as their burdens become too much to bear and with no one there to help them.

When they cried to God in their day of distress, his light penetrated the darkness and demolished their shackles. Then he set them free and gave them hope. Do you feel as though you are imprisoned by the past? You may be hopelessly thinking that there is no way out of your dilemma. Are haunting regrets increasingly suffocating your soul as you endeavor to simply survive yet another day of existence? Do you sense that your life is slowly slipping away as you drift apart from any prospects of help? God is beseeching you right now, "Come to me. I will rescue you!" Turn this day of distress into the day of deliverance! God is faithful to his promises.

God is beseeching you right now, "Come to me. I will rescue you!" Turn this day of distress into the day of deliverance!

As this Psalm continues unfolding, verse 17 depicts the foolish who have mocked the wisdom of God. Their sins festered into sorrow and misery, eventually affecting their health. Even the suggestion of food seemed loathsome to them. They cried out to God in their day of trouble as death knocked at their door. He sent his word, healed them and delivered them from their destructions.

It is possible that you knew God more intimately at one time, but because of unresolved disappointments reinforced by the deceitful influences of the world, you turned your back on him and are now anguished, but you can't find your way back. God hasn't turned his back on you. God promises to send his powerful and personal word to you. That word may come as a still small voice in the night, a dream or vision, through reading the Scriptures or spoken by an inspired messenger. Whatever way it is delivered, that word from God will heal you and pull you back from the brink of destruction. Once again you will discover his goodness through the revelation of his love for you. As you reach for the torch of freedom, you will light your way back to the relationship with God for which you were designed and intended. There is a Psalm that says, "He lifted me out of the pit of despair, out of the mud and the mire. He set my feet on solid ground and steadied me as I walked along."[7] This verse encourages us that God can dynamically change our lives. One minute we are in a quagmire; the next, he lifts us to a secure place of stability and clear direction.

Psalm 107:23 then speaks of those who set sail to do trade in a foreign land. As the seas became stormy and the waves threatened their lives, their souls melted from distress. But when they literally sent out a "distress signal" to God, he calmed the raging seas and quieted their hearts. Then their cries of despair turned into shouts of praise and joy as he brought them into a peaceful harbor. Perhaps you are a businessperson who has sailed into an uncharted territory and find yourself in a season where everything around you is turbulent. As your heart sinks within you, you lament, *This is it. Time to close the doors!* Send out an SOS to God and watch him still the storm, turn the tide, hush the rough waters of calamity and guide you into your sheltered sanctuary and port of peace. Another Psalm concurs that God is the one "who stills the roaring of the seas, the roaring of their waves, the tumult of the peoples."[8] Are you ready to calm the commotion in your life? No matter who you are or where you have been, God will partner with you and bring you to untroubled waters.

After each scenario is presented in Psalm 107, the pattern is summarized; "Then they cry unto the LORD in their trouble, and he brings them out of their distresses.... Oh that men would praise the LORD for his goodness, and for his wonderful works to the children of men!" Psalm 107 culminates with, "Whoever is wise, let him give heed to these things; let men consider the steadfast love of the LORD." This exhortation has the flavor of pausing in the presence of God. Selah![9]

Our response to God's invitation to overcome stress through his presence brings blessings, not only into our lives but to those around us also. Our decision whether or not to go to him affects our family, friends, colleagues and community. Now we will look into the life of King Jehoshaphat and discover how his habit of going to God, in his day of distress, rescued him and caused an entire nation to prosper.

References:

1. Psalm 73:1-3 (NIV); verses 4 and 5 (TPT); Psalm 73:6-11 (NLT); Psalm 73:13 (TPT); Psalm 73:14 (Multiple versions); Psalm 73:15-16 (MSG); Psalms 73:17 (NLT); Psalm 73:18-20 (MSG) Psalm 73:21-24 (NLT) and Psalm 73:25-28

2. Psalm 77:2a (TPT); Psalm 77:3 and Psalm 77:4 (TLB)

3. Proverbs 13:12 (TPT)

4. Zephaniah 3:17 (NLT)

5. Psalm 77:7-9 (TLB); Psalm 77:10 (GNT); Psalm 77:11 (NIV) and referenced from Psalm 77:11-15

6. Proverbs 3:5-6 (AMP)

7. Psalm 40:2 (NLT)

8. Psalm 65:7 (ESV)

9. Referenced from Psalm 107

CHAPTER 7

HOW JEHOSHAPHAT WAS RESCUED FROM STRESS

Life is a series of peaks and valleys. It is likely you have journeyed through seasons of vibrant health and increasing prosperity, where the days of peace are as quiet as a cricket chirping on a summer evening. It's easy to praise God when everything is going great, but where does your heart go when sudden and disturbing news interrupts your stability and threatens all you are and everything you have?

That was exactly what happened to King Jehoshaphat. He was faced with a decision that not only affected his personal life, but everyone in Judah. The Moabites, Ammonites and others joined forces to conquer Jehoshaphat's kingdom. They were spotted approaching from the southeast while still approximately thirty miles away. The invaders were maneuvering through an almost impossible terrain of jagged mountains and sheer cliffs with a strategy to catch the people of Judah off guard. These enemies were not planning on returning home. They carried all their possessions and treasures with the purpose of permanently settling down in Jerusalem, the capital of Judah. When the scout's startling report reached the ears of Jehoshaphat, he surmised that in about fifteen hours, his kingdom might be destroyed. Before the next nightfall, the king and his people could be drawing their last breath before being executed, or alternatively, living out the rest of their lives in slavery.[1]

Jehoshaphat was afraid. Previously, he had been rebuked by the prophet Jehu, who warned him that God was not pleased with his love and alliance to those who hated the Lord.[2] Ironically, Jehoshaphat's father, Asa, received a similar reproof from Jehu's father, the prophet Hanani, years earlier.[3] Maybe the guilt of these previous incidents fueled Jehoshaphat's fear. While he could have buckled under the enormous pressure, Jehoshaphat positioned his heart toward God instead. He proclaimed a fast throughout the land for his people to pursue God with all of their hearts. This fast involved the abstinence of food, but more importantly it was a deliberate plan to humbly and reverently focus on God for help. A true fast triggered by calamity takes precedence over any other activity and centers its attention solely on God. All the people throughout Judah gathered to Jerusalem and sought God's direction for this life or death situation.

...where does your heart go when sudden and disturbing news interrupts your stability and threatens all you are and everything you have?

THE PRAYER OF JEHOSHAPHAT

Jehoshaphat stood in the house of the Lord before the assembly and opened with praise:

"O Lord God of our ancestors, you are the God who lives in heaven and rules over all the kingdoms of the nations. You possess strength and power; no one can stand against you. Our God, you drove out the inhabitants of this land before your people Israel and gave it as a permanent possession to the descendants of your friend Abraham. They settled down in it and built a temple to honor you, saying, 'If disaster comes on us in the form of military attack, judgment, plague, or famine, we will stand in front of this temple before you, for you are present in this temple. We will cry out to you for help in our distress, so that you will hear and deliver us.' Now the Ammonites, Moabites, and men from Mount Seir are coming! When Israel came from the land of Egypt, you did not allow them to invade these lands. They bypassed them and did not destroy them. Look how they are repaying us! They come to drive us out of our allotted land which you assigned to us! Our God, will you not judge them? For we are powerless against this huge army that attacks us! We don't know what we should do; we look to you for help."[4]

Jehoshaphat insisted that the whole country join him in the *God Place*. He began his prayer by reminding God that it was God himself who made covenant promises with Abraham, Isaac and Jacob, and that he is in heaven ruling over earthly kingdoms with power and might. God already knew all of these things, of course, but Jehoshaphat acknowledged the Lord for who he declared himself to be. This praise knit together the hearts of all of the people and began to shift their attention toward the *God Place*. As Jehoshaphat continued his prayer, he pointed out that God gave the land to his friend Abraham and his descendants to dwell in forever. He recalled the historical dedication of the temple by Solomon, David's son, where the presence of God was represented and honored. At that time, Solomon declared to God, "If your people Israel are defeated before the enemy because they have sinned against you, and they turn again and acknowledge your name and pray and plead with you in this house, then hear from heaven and forgive the sin of your people Israel and bring them again to the land that you gave to them and to their fathers."[5]

Jehoshaphat continued his persuasive prayer to God: "You gave us this inheritance. It is your possession. Are you going to let our enemies take it away? Judge them!" Then followed the most remarkable part of the prayer. Jehoshaphat cried out, "For we are powerless against this huge army that attacks us! We don't know what we should do; we look to you for help."

In this narrative, we once again see God's well-defined pattern for being rescued from stress. Jehoshaphat's story teaches us that in times of trouble and days of distress to pray the declarations of God with confidence and remind him of his promises to us. We should speak boldly, "When I cry out to you in my distress, you will hear me and save me. I am powerless against what is coming against me. I don't know what I should do; I look to you for help." This humble appeal emphasizes that our wisdom, resources and abilities are useless against the problems we face. We don't know how to deal with them because we were never designed by our Creator to handle stress without his intervention. When the pressures of life seem to be insurmountable, that's when we fix our eyes on God and all he declares himself to be.

All of Judah stood before the Lord. They deliberately placed the wives, children and babies out front to assure that God would recognize their frailty and have mercy on them. Then the Spirit of the Lord came upon Jahaziel, a descendant of Asaph.

He said, "Listen, all Judah, the people of Jerusalem, and King Jehoshaphat. The Lord says to you, 'Do not be afraid or troubled because of these many men. For the battle is not yours but God's. Go down to fight them tomorrow. See, they will come up by the hill of Ziz. You will find them at the end of the valley in front of the desert of Jeruel. You will not need to fight in this battle. Just stand still in your places and see the saving power of the Lord work for you, O Judah and Jerusalem.' Do not be afraid or troubled. Go out against them tomorrow, for the Lord is with you."[6]

Jahaziel's exclamation from God is reminiscent of a familiar verse: "Be still, and know that I am God."[7] A good rendering of this verse (compiled from different translations) is; "Cease and desist from your own strength and efforts, and taste, see and experience that I am your God." Can you hear him personally imploring you right now? This same exhortation has been declared to millions of "whoevers" throughout the world and over the centuries. Make this your personal directive also. God's promises to us still ring loudly, including: "Don't be afraid, for I am with you; don't be distressed, for I am your God. I give you strength, I give you help, I support you with my victorious right hand," and "Be strong. Take courage. Don't be intimidated. Don't give them a second thought because God, your God, is striding ahead of you. He's right there with you. He won't let you down; he won't leave you."[8]

As Jehoshaphat heard these declarations, he responded with humility and bowed with his face to the ground. Those assembled with the king followed suit and dropped to their knees in worship.[9] Worshiping God fosters a humble recognition of how insignificant we are while acknowledging how awesome he is. It is a vital aspect of the *God Place*. We need to guard both the purity and the priority of true worship in our lives.

Many years after the life of King Jehoshaphat, the worship of God had degraded into a ceremonial ritual. In an attempt to call the people back to genuinely worshiping God, the prophet Isaiah spoke this admonishment. "The Lord said, 'These people claim to worship me, but their words are meaningless, and their hearts are somewhere else. Their religion is nothing but human rules and traditions, which they have simply memorized.'"[10] Isaiah later relayed that their fasting was an act of self-righteousness. They hoped God might take notice and reward their outward appearances and efforts. Yet God did not accept their gestures because their hearts were not in it. (Again, remember that God looks on the heart.) Through the prophet Isaiah, God told the people to turn from doing their own pleasure on his holy day. Alternatively, they were to honor him by not doing *their own ways*, neither *finding their own pleasure*, nor *speaking their own words*, but by delighting themselves in him.[11] "Delight" means to *luxuriate in*. The Bible says that God delights in our obedience more than offerings and sacrifices.[12] Humankind tends to place value on outward appearances, but God treasures our loving submission:

doing what he requests no matter how small or insignificant it may appear. Our obedience to God should always be from the heart and never out of obligation.

As mentioned earlier, after Jehu had reproved Jehoshaphat, the king repented and began to further prepare his heart to seek God. There is a difference between seeking God and preparing our hearts to seek him. Preparing our hearts entails getting rid of the things that preclude us from seeking God. This may include unfruitful commitments and activities, extraneous busyness, destructive relationships and other distractions. The Scriptures inform us that when people prepared their hearts to seek God, it often involved the removal of idols from their lives. As Jehoshaphat prepared his heart, he also appointed judges and Levitical priests over cities in Judah and commanded those officials to faithfully conduct themselves with reverence and loyalty to God in their hearts. The whole country was influenced by their example, and Jehoshaphat's decision to seek God instilled the same heartfelt allegiance into the culture of Judah.[13]

> *There is a difference between seeking God and preparing our hearts to seek him.*

The consistent planting and cultivating of the seeds of God's goodness, power and love established a trust among the people to seek him with confident expectation in the face of opposition. As they encountered their stressful dilemma, their prepared hearts naturally responded by going to God for help because their relationship with him was rooted in his promise to rescue them. This is a great benefit of taking time to prepare our hearts—it incites us to look to God instead of overreacting to troublesome events with our own limited solutions.

Then the appointed ministers of music stood up and began to praise God with a great and loud voice. Praise engages the heart and ushers it into the *God Place* by giving thanks to him for what he has done, what he is doing and what he will do. Praise directs our eyes away from the problem and onto the problem solver.

Early the next morning, the inhabitants of Judah and Jerusalem rose up with obedient anticipation to carry out God's instructions. Jehoshaphat boldly stood before the congregation and proclaimed, "Listen to me! Believe and trust in the Lord your God and you will be secure. Believe and trust also in his prophets and you will prosper and succeed." Then the king chose musicians to go before the army, singing praises and giving thanks to God because his lovingkindness continues forever." As they broke into joyful song and praise, God set ambushes against those who had joined forces to come against Judah. God launched his victorious plan of deliverance at the very moment the people started praising him! Judah's adversaries became confused and ended up fighting themselves. The battle escalated and the suspicion of betrayal prompted the enemy's total annihilation of each other. Judah stood still, looked on, and with awe witnessed the swift and mighty hand of God. As he moved, he fulfilled his promises of victory, prosperity and success. When the battle was over, dead bodies were strewn about the land. Not one foe was left standing. The treasures, garments and other valuable things that the enemy initially brought with them (with the intent of permanently settling in Jerusalem) were now scattered as far as the eye could see. It took the people of Judah three days to gather the riches. Even then, there was still more than they could possibly carry away! Not only did they experience the spiritual benefit of obeying God by gaining a massive military triumph, they also received a splendid material token of his abundant provision.

Praise directs our eyes away from the problem and onto the problem solver.

On the fourth day, the people of Judah assembled in the Valley of Berachah (meaning *blessing*, because there they blessed and praised God). Joyfully parading back to Jerusalem, they sang and played musical instruments the entire way and entered into the temple. He caused them to rejoice over their enemies, and when the surrounding countries heard what God had done, great awe and reverence swept over them. Then Jehoshaphat's kingdom was quiet as God gave them rest.[14]

DECISIONS IN LIGHT OF OTHERS

This remarkable account of Jehoshaphat teaches us that our decisions, especially in time of distress, will have an influence on our households, families, neighborhoods, communities and nations. It is sobering to realize how our choices impact so many others through our relationships. Like a stone tossed into still waters, our decisions ripple out and dramatically affect those whose lives are connected to ours. Jehoshaphat's story also encourages us to stay humble, keep our hearts pure, and seek the Lord in our *God Place* with genuine praise and worship, both in good times and in times of calamity. Whatever God instructs us to do, we are to carry it out and stay faithful to him—for he is faithful to us!

In the next chapter, we will conclude our observations of how people dealt with their times of trouble by discovering the secret to Jesus Christ's victory over an unfathomable level of stress during his last few days on earth.

References
1.   Referenced from 2 Chronicles 20:1-2
2.   2 Chronicles 19:2
3.   2 Chronicles 16:7
4.   2 Chronicles 20:6-12 (NET)
5.   2 Chronicles 6:24-25 (ESV)
6.   2 Chronicles 20:15-17 (NLV)
7.   Psalm 46:10a
8.   Isaiah 41:10 (CJB) and Deuteronomy 31:6 (MSG)
9.   2 Chronicles 20:18
10. Isaiah 29:13 (GNT)
11. Isaiah 58:13-14
12. 1 Samuel 15:22
13. 2 Chronicles 19:4-11
14. 2 Chronicles 20:19-21 (Referenced from multiple versions)

CHAPTER 8

HOW JESUS WAS RESCUED FROM STRESS

Volumes have been written about Jesus Christ, the Son of God. However, few address the manner in which he handled the stress of going to the cross and laying down his life for all humankind. He was sent to be the Savior of the world. The world needed a Savior because of Adam and Eve's transgression and the loss of spirit life (as discussed near the close of Chapter 2). After the fall of Adam and Eve, God immediately promised that the seed of a woman was going to ultimately destroy the works of the devil. Old Testament prophecies revealed the coming of a Messiah and Redeemer who would restore spirit life back to God's created beings. Additionally, the dominion over God's creation that had been transferred from Adam to Satan would be recovered.

As a Jewish boy, Jesus learned the Old Testament Scriptures and saw the prophecies which outlined his purpose, life, death and even his resurrection. Yet his vast knowledge of the Scriptures never took the place of a relationship with his heavenly Father. Isaiah prophesied that Jesus would be a servant of God who acted wisely and "astonished many" when they saw him. During his crucifixion he was beaten so badly that he no longer resembled a human being.[1] Isaiah revealed many details of Jesus' destiny: "But he was pierced for our transgressions; he was crushed for our iniquities; upon him was the chastisement that brought us peace, and with his wounds we are healed."[2]

Jesus, the servant of God, died for every sin and sickness on our behalf. He took all of our stress upon himself at the cross. The chastisement for our peace and wholeness was upon him. ("Chastisement" in this verse refers to the instructional discipline that Jesus received from his heavenly Father in order to endure all mental and emotional afflictions in our stead.)

During the time of Jesus Christ's earthly ministry, the religious leaders taught their self-conceived traditions and presented them as the word of God. As a result, these doctrines nullified the covenant promises of God, and as Isaiah had warned, these leaders honored God with their lips, but their hearts were far from him. As Jesus began to travel through the villages, preaching, teaching and healing all that came to him, he looked upon the condition of the flocks of people before him, and his loving empathy for them was ignited. The Gospel of Matthew vividly describes the state of God's people. "But when he saw the multitudes, he was moved with compassion for them, because they were distressed and scattered, as sheep not having a shepherd."[3] The description of the words "distressed" and "scattered" paint the picture of God's people being harassed, weary, bewildered and cast down as though neglected. Today we might use the phrase, "coming apart at the seams." On the outside, they appeared as a normal, everyday population who attended their synagogue faithfully on the Sabbath and observed all the religious customs. They were taught the Old Testament Scriptures and attempted to carry out the commandments of God. But inside they were helpless, hopeless and disheartened.

> *Outward conformity gains its strength by producing an appearance of change, yet the heart is not genuinely affected.*

Worldly traditions are still being propounded from various

places where conformity to the rules and behavior modification are presented as the requirement for being approved and accepted by God. Even now, many gatherings in the name of the Lord are nothing more than social corrals of comparison, self-righteousness and judgment. The subtlety lies in the good intentions of others who feel it is their place and even their responsibility to keep others accountable. Outward conformity gains its strength by producing an appearance of change, yet the heart is not genuinely affected. Human-driven religious practice produces the same level of distress now as it did in Jesus' day. Millions go through the rituals of honoring God with their lips, but their hearts have wandered from him because the message they hear is laced with the leaven of legalism; they feel they can never measure up to receive the goodness and love of God. This topic will be further addressed in a later chapter.

We will be delivered from much distress as we return to God's true words once again rather than subjecting ourselves to the doctrines of pseudo-religious and human tradition. Jesus Christ is the promised good shepherd to lead us back to our Creator. How did Jesus care for his flock, God's people? The book of Acts says he "began to do and teach."[4] His example modeled the sequence of *doing* first, then *teaching*.

Jesus was not exempted from the things he spoke from God. For example, he taught, "Therefore do not worry about tomorrow, for tomorrow will worry about its own things. Sufficient for the day is its own trouble."[5] He practiced them in his own life. This was evident in how he responded to the events leading up to his death.

The night Jesus was betrayed was the first time we see him confronting an immense amount of distress. He entered into the garden of Gethsemane with his disciples and told them to sit, while he went and prayed. Then he began to be sorrowful and troubled. Distress and anguish weighed him down as he envisioned the reality of the events that were about to occur. He then instructed Peter,

James and John to remain and watch, but even those closest to him could not stand with him in this dark hour. Jesus went further into the garden alone. He fell face down on the ground and prayed, "Abba, Father, all things are possible for you. Remove this cup from me. Yet not what I will, but what you will."[6]

The degree of stress at this moment in Jesus' life was almost unbearable. Under this exceeding pressure, he sought God his Father and asked if there was any way that the suffering to come could be avoided. The "cup" figuratively represented the excruciating and agonizing events surrounding the crucifixion. There he would experience immense affliction as he took upon himself the sins and sicknesses of the world. The mental pressure of interrogation, mockery, rejection and accusation turned out to be as intense as the physical torture. He became the lowest in order to identify with and save the very least of any man, woman, or child. His broken body healed our diseases. His external wounds paid the price for our external sins while his internal bruises dealt with our internal sins. He took on our stress to bring us peace and soundness of mind.

As he prayed, Jesus referred to God as *Abba*, an intimate, endearing and respectful term for "my Father," and declared, "All things are possible for you." Jesus fervently cried out these words as portrayed by the gospel of Luke during the intensity of his prayer. "And there appeared to him an angel from heaven, strengthening him. And being in agony he prayed more earnestly; and his sweat became like great drops of blood falling down to the ground."[7] While it is medically possible to sweat blood, it is extremely rare. The word "like" in this verse indicates a figure of speech: the sweating of blood is a representation of the intensity he poured into this prayer.

Psalm 22 vividly depicts Jesus' mental and physical trauma during the crucifixion:

"I am poured out like water, and all my bones are out of joint; my heart is like wax; it is melted within my breast; my strength is dried up like a potsherd, and my tongue sticks to my jaws; you lay me in the dust of death. For dogs encompass me; a company of evildoers encircles me; they have pierced my hands and feet—I can count all my bones—they stare and gloat over me; they divide my garments among them, and for my clothing they cast lots."[8]

Christ repeated his request that the cup pass from him three times. It is clear that he did not want to go through with the crucifixion and sought another way. Still, he thoroughly understood from the Old Testament Scriptures that it was God's will for him to be crucified. He told his disciples previously on numerous occasions that he must suffer, die and on the third day rise again. Even during the week before going to the cross, stress attempted to knock at the door of his soul, but he did not yield to it by giving it any further attention. He practiced what he taught: "Don't worry about tomorrow."

He became the lowest in order to identify with and save the very least of any man, woman, or child.

THE BOSOM OF THE FATHER

If Jesus knew the will of God was for him to die, why did he pray so passionately to be delivered from that horrifying event? How could this incredible man seem to be conceding to the crushing weight of sacrificing his life and pleading with his Father for a way out? The answer lies in the declared truth of Jesus' total dependence upon his Father God. He faithfully disclosed that, "He could do nothing of himself . . . only what he saw his Father doing" and "He could do nothing on his own . . . only what he heard."[9] He lived from the bosom of his Father.

The bosom is the deepest and most intimate region of the *God*

97

Place. It depicts several things. The "bosom of a father" is well known to many cultures. It is likened to the folds in loose garments that are worn over the upper body and that extend over the lap. Fathers carry their children in the bosom and drape the folds over the child to support its weight and to provide protection from the sun or other harsh elements. Shepherds adopted this gentle practice to tenderly transport their young and dependent lambs as well. The bosom is not just exclusive to babies. Both youth and adults also lean into another's bosom as a gesture of close friendship and trust. The bosom represented stability, confirmation, safety, soothing comfort and reliability. One who exhibited this affectionate and watchful care over their child was called a "nursing father" and the young one could hear and feel the strong heartbeat of its father while it was in the bosom and carried about. Fathers especially delighted in having a son because in that culture, a male child was groomed to learn his father's business, carry out responsibilities as an heir and continue the legacy and namesake of the family.

In certain cultures artisans have guarded their skills like a sacred trust for centuries, especially in countries where machinery and automation have not gained popularity. The art and craftsmanship of many trades have long been preserved by being handed down from father to son. The closest secrets of the trades such as a woodworker, jeweler or metalsmith are confidentially passed along from generation to generation. When a non-family member desires to learn a trade or art, they must apprentice for years without pay to acquire their skills through working and practicing under supervision. The master never reveals the secrets of his trade to outsiders until they serve out their time and have proven to be worthy of his confidence and favor. Some apprentices who are not loyal to their masters depart from their training without ever learning the revered details which add a valuable distinction to their work of art and fetch a higher price in the marketplace.

The relationship with a father and his son is different. He eats with his father, works with him in the field, and at the shop, and shares his life from the outset. It is common for the father-son relationship to begin at birth, and for that bond to grow strong as the son is "in the bosom of the father." In the shop, the father mixes formulas and finishes objects behind closed doors in the presence of his son. The apprentices and other workers are not allowed to see these intricate processes. But the father shares all that he knows and allows his son to practice on objects that an apprentice is not allowed to touch. The father instructs his son with gentleness and patience, hoping someday to hand over to him the family business so that it continues into future generations.[10]

In the same way Jesus did not primarily gain his knowledge from books, schools, rabbis or priests, but from a relationship with his heavenly Father. He even told his earthly parents, "I must be about my Father's business."[11] Although prophets and priests were chosen to learn and communicate the truths of God, they rarely saw, heard or grasped the deep and hidden things of God's heart; they were apprentices. Jesus Christ is the only begotten son of God. His heavenly Father revealed his heart to his son and instructed him in wisdom, knowledge and understanding. God and his son were in constant communion. They kept nothing back from each other. That is why Jesus explained that he saw, heard and did what his Father intended for him to carry out. He and his heavenly Father were one. They worked in harmony while sharing the same purpose of heart.

In previous chapters we have surveyed the lives of great believers who, when under stress, went to their *God Place* and sought the Lord for deliverance. Now we discover Jesus Christ doing the very same thing. Shouldn't we also follow in the footsteps of those who demonstrated how to be rescued from their times of trouble and days of distress?

Did God answer his son's prayer in the garden? The book of Hebrews tells us, "While Jesus was here on earth, he offered prayers and pleadings, with a loud cry and tears, to the one who could rescue him from death. And God heard his prayers because of his deep reverence for God."[12] Recall that when the Bible says God hears, it means he *answers*. The answer wasn't through the angel sent to the garden as mentioned previously, because Jesus remained in agony even after that visitation. The evidence of his answered prayer is revealed when Jesus emerged from the garden and confidently announced, "Do you think I cannot call on my Father, and he will at once put at my disposal more than twelve legions of angels? But how then would the Scriptures be fulfilled that say it must happen in this way?" and, "Shall I not drink the cup the Father has given me?" and also, "A time is coming and in fact has come when you will be scattered, each to your own home. You will leave me all alone. Yet I am not alone, for my Father is with me."[13] Jesus progressed from his weakness and reluctance of having to face the cross to a courageous position of confidence. Now he was fully prepared to fulfill his purpose and exchange his life for all of humankind. He did not rely solely upon his scriptural knowledge to get him through this historical event. He completely leaned upon the bosom of his heavenly Father.

THE JOYFUL ANSWER

What exactly was God's answer to Jesus' prayer? It is also recorded in Hebrews. "Looking steadfastly on Jesus the leader and completer of faith: who, in view of the joy lying before him, endured the cross, having despised the shame, and is set down at the right hand of the throne of God." The answer was the *joy* laid before him. Oh, how powerful joy can be in our times of stress! The Bible says that in the presence of God, or before his face, is "the fulness of joy."[14]

Joy was the answer to Jesus' stress surrounding the events of the cross. This mighty wave of joy washed over the shame of the cross and brought an enduring realization of accomplishing God's will. As Jesus felt his life fading away, he said, "It is finished!" He knew by revelation that he would soon be in the presence of his Father, experiencing the fullness of joy forever. God fulfilled his promise and raised his son from the dead. Soon thereafter, Jesus ascended to the Father where God made him both Lord and Christ. Today he sits at the right hand of God! God will also fulfill all his promises to you!

> *Joy was the answer to Jesus' stress surrounding the events of the cross.*

Perhaps you need a different answer to your stress right now. Maybe you need peace, love, kindness, healing or finances. Whatever it is, go to God in your time of stress and he *will* become your deliverance. God is so concerned about you as his child that he will give you *exactly* what you need, including the right answer and direction in which to move.

While visiting India many years ago, I was awakened early one morning by vendors pushing their carts through the narrow streets and calling out an invitation to buy their goods. About this same time, I gained a deeper understanding of a passage from Isaiah, "Ho, everyone who thirsts, come to the water, and you who have no money, come, buy and eat. Come, buy wine and milk without money and without cost! Why spend your money on food that doesn't give you strength? Why pay for groceries that do you no good? Listen and I'll tell you where to get good food that fattens up the soul!"[15]

What did Isaiah mean when he said, "Come, buy wine and milk without money and without cost?" How can someone purchase these items without currency or knowing the price? Looking through the lens of the customs in the lands and times of the Bible reveals that the invitation was extended by street merchants. Many poor people could not afford these things, but occasionally wealthy people celebrated their birthdays by giving a gift to others while expressing their thankfulness to God for living another year. These benefactors often bought all of the water, wine and milk, and then had the merchant distribute it for free. This was a way celebrants could express their gratitude for life by quenching the thirst of others and thereby giving them life, gladness, and nourishment.

These verses are a prophecy regarding the Lord Jesus Christ. He paid the price for *every* "whoever" since we could never afford the price of salvation and redemption. It is impossible to even begin to cover the cost of cleansing ourselves from sin or gaining acceptance from God. Yet he calls out to us, "Come and receive! The price for your salvation has been paid!" These verses question why we try to accomplish this by our own works, and then reiterate his invitation to us: "Why spend your money on food that doesn't give you strength? Why pay for groceries that do you no good? Listen and I'll tell you where to get good food that fattens up the soul!" The epistle to the Romans extends this greatest of invitations to "whoever." "That if you confess with your mouth Jesus as Lord, and believe in your heart that God raised Him from the dead, you will be saved; for with the heart a person believes, resulting in righteousness, and with the mouth he confesses, resulting in salvation."[16] This is not some tagline or easy formula to salvation. It is a deliberate decision of the heart where you realize there is someone and something greater than you and outside yourself, and you respond by submitting your life to another.

> Salvation is God's answer to every problem you will encounter.

Are you tired of trying to be your own lord? Why not accept this invitation to salvation both now and for all eternity? Salvation includes wholeness, healing, protection, safety and the rescuing from destruction. Salvation is God's answer to every problem you will encounter. More importantly, it involves the release from stress and the slavery of sin.

Let's discover how God brings this miraculous deliverance into our lives.

References:

1. Isaiah 52:13-14

2. Isaiah 53:5 (ESV)

3. Matthew 9:36 (ASV)

4. Acts 1:1

5. Matthew 6:34

6. Mark 14:36 (ESV)

7. Luke 22:43-44 (ESV)

8. Psalm 22:14-18 (ESV)

9. Referenced from John 5:19 and 5:30a

10. Lamsa, George M., Gospel Light, A revised and edited and annotated with supporting scholarly references and footnotes.(Nebraska: The Aramaic Bible Society, Morris Publishing, 1999), 423-424; Freeman, James M., Manners and Customs of the Bible, (New Jersey: Bridge Publishing Co.), 273 and Pillai, K.C., website: www.biblecustoms.org.

11. Luke 2:49

12. Hebrews 5:7 (NLT)

13. Matthew 26:53-54 (NIV); John 18:11b (NIV) and John 16:32 (NIV)

14. Hebrews 12:2. (DBY) and Psalm 16:11

15. Isaiah 55:1-2 (TLB)

16. Romans 10:9 and 10 (NASB)

CHAPTER 9

THE BLOOD AND THE CROSS

Sin-consciousness is one of life's major causes of stress. It drastically debilitates every person and consequently moves us away from God's presence. This separation from the presence of God hinders our ability to see who we really are and blurs our understanding of our true value and purpose in life. God's love toward us does not vary, but our perception of the reality of his love becomes distorted as we focus on our sin-consciousness. We learned earlier that being self-focused was never God's intention or design for his glorious created beings. In fact, it was self-focus and the temptation to be independent from God that brought about the fall of the human race.

Since the garden of Eden, human beings have been consumed and distracted with the never-ending quest to find their value and purpose in life. But God increases an awareness and hunger for more of him, and through his gentle goodness, he brings us to the point of realizing the emptiness of a self-centered life. This realization is an awakening that causes us to seek something much greater than ourselves—namely God as our heavenly Father and Jesus Christ as our Lord and Savior. We are compelled to explore our value and purpose through a relationship with God the Father and the Son, a relationship governed by love, grace and goodness. This is good news!

The Bible identifies Satan as the "god of this world" who blinds people from seeing the light of the good news.[1] Satan attempts to promote a culture where the influences of self-perception, mingled with discrete judgements from others, determine our worth. Consequently, a false identity begins to take shape through self-contemplation and unsolicited evaluations by others. If we allow that illusory identity to overshadow the reality of who God has truly made us to be, then his purpose for our lives is thwarted. Under this distorted estimation, our self-worth becomes defined by our performance rather than our identity. Performance should follow identity: not the other way around. Comparing ourselves with others puts our lives in chaotic and stressful disarray. We will find ourselves judging others while trying to increase our value by demeaning the value of those around us.

Because God is love, he relentlessly searched for us when we were lost and paid the highest price to bring us back to the glorious dignity and worthiness which he always intended for his creation. As we come to truly *experience* God's assessment of us, our attention turns from ourselves to our Creator, and we live through the mindset of his value and purpose for our lives.

> *Performance should follow identity: not the other way around.*

A SOLUTION TO THE SIN PROBLEM: THE BLOOD

One way to define sin is "our declared independence from God." The result of sin is shame, and shame leads to our distress. (Again: God does not diminish his everlasting love to us, but our hearts register a sense of guilt often inflamed by the deceitful schemes of the devil.) Because all were born from the bloodline of Adam, we were all born sinners because we inherited Adam's nature and identity. This means we didn't *become* sinners because we sinned; we sinned because we were *already* sinners. It was our nature.

During the days of Moses, God established the Old Testament covenant with the children of Israel. This covenant contained laws to protect the people and dealt with the covering of their sins through the rituals and rites of a priest who was assigned to represent the people before God. The priest ceremoniously sacrificed animals; the shedding of the animal's blood was a substitute representing the life of the animal in exchange for the life of the people. This sacrificial act was a metaphor, a shadow of the promise of the coming Messiah, Jesus, who was to lay down his righteous life in exchange for our sinful lives.

But why blood? The Old Testament explains, "For the life of the flesh is in the blood, and I have given it to you upon the altar to make atonement for your souls; for it is the blood that makes atonement for the soul."[2] On a specific day each year (called the Day of Atonement), the high priest offered a special sacrifice that was different from other sacrifices. It served to consolidate all the daily offerings from the past year into one distinctive offering. The priest chose two unblemished goats. He laid his hands on the head of the one goat chosen for death and confessed the sins of the people. They watched as the animal was slaughtered and its life was poured out in exchange for theirs. Next, the high priest entered the innermost sacred place of the sanctuary, the "Holy of Holies." It was the only time of the year when he accessed this place. There he sprinkled the blood on the "mercy seat" which was part of the lid that covered the Ark of the Covenant. Here, on one special day each year, in this sacred and secluded place, God met the high priest, the lone representative of the people. God saw the sprinkled blood and covered their sins for another year.

The high priest then took the other goat that had not been chosen for sacrifice, and in full view of the people laid his hands on the head of the animal, symbolically transferring the sins of the people onto it, and sent it into the wilderness. The expression "scapegoat" comes from this practice. This act represented that their sins were gone from the eyes of God. The book of Hebrews affirms, "If they could have, one offering would have been enough; the worshipers would have been cleansed once for all, and their feeling of guilt would be gone....But just the opposite happened: those yearly sacrifices reminded them of their disobedience and guilt instead of relieving their minds ... Under the old agreement the priests stood before the altar day after day offering sacrifices that could never take away our sins. But Christ gave himself to God for our sins as one sacrifice for all time and then sat down in the place of highest honor at God's right hand."[3] Hebrews is teaching us that while priests under the Old Covenant offered many sacrifices for sins, Jesus, as the high priest of the New Covenant, offered one sacrifice for all sins through the shedding of his blood on the cross. His one sacrifice lasts forever.

How valuable is the blood of Christ? Romans tells us that through the blood we "are justified by his grace as a gift, through the redemption that is in Christ Jesus, whom God put forward as a propitiation by his blood, to be received by faith. This was to show God's righteousness, because in his divine forbearance he had passed over former sins."[4] There are four vital words in this passage. *Justified* means to be acquitted, as though a judge handed down a verdict and proclaimed, "Not guilty!" *Grace* is God's undeserved favor given freely and not earned by any works we perform. *Redemption* pertains to the liberation of someone through a payment. *Propitiation* is the same word translated elsewhere as "mercy seat," so God set forth Jesus to be the mercy seat through faith in his blood. God fully accepted and is totally pleased with Christ's sacrifice. Ephesians proclaims, "For by the blood of Christ we are set free, that is, our sins are forgiven. How great is the grace of God."[5]

This forgiveness of our sins results in a huge release of stress because it takes care of our guilt and shame once and for all. The first epistle of John exhorts, "On the other hand, if we walk in the light as He is, *then* in the light we have fellowship with one another, and the blood of Jesus, His Son, cleanses us from every sin."[6] Notice that it is not only that the blood cleansed the sins we committed *before* we were saved, but it *continues* to cleanse us from all sins present and future. Furthermore, the first epistle of Peter (1:18-19) declares, "You know that a price was paid to redeem you from following the empty ways handed on to you by your ancestors; it was not paid with things that perish (like silver and gold), but with the precious blood of the Anointed, who was like a perfect and unblemished sacrificial lamb."[7] The blood of Christ is precious—and you are redeemed with that blood. Imagine, then, how precious you are to God! Your worth is not determined by the world or by any human being including yourself. It is determined by the price that was paid for you. That price is the very life of God's only begotten Son.

The divine constant that never changes is that we are saved through the blood of Jesus Christ and our faith in him. Despite this, we are often conscious of our sin and therefore experience guilt and shame: we feel unworthy. Yet because of the blood of Christ, we are not to accept sin-consciousness any longer! If you sense a wall between yourself and God or feel you do not deserve his presence, ask him to enlighten your heart! He will give you understanding so you can know—and receive the assurance—that the wall has been taken down. The tearing down of this wall means that your access to the *God Place* is not based on your behavior, good deeds or level of participation in godly activities. Your access is solely through the sacrifice of Jesus so that, "Now because of Christ—dying that death, shedding that blood—you who were once out of it altogether are in on everything."[8]

> *The blood of Christ is precious—and you are redeemed with that blood. Imagine, then, how precious you are to God!*

The devil will constantly try to point out our weaknesses and failures (one of names the Bible uses to refer to the devil is *the accuser*[9]). But when he attempts to do this, we should simply tell him that he has no ground to stand on. We should declare, "If the blood of Christ is good enough for God, then the blood of Christ is good enough for me! That's my story and I'm sticking with it!"

The book of Romans expresses this same idea: "But God shows his love for us in that while we were still sinners, Christ died for us. Since, therefore, we have now been justified by his blood, much more shall we be saved by him from the wrath of God. For if while we were enemies we were reconciled to God by the death of his Son, much more, now that we are reconciled, shall we be saved by his life."[10] "Reconciled" means to *reconnect something that was once separated.* We were once separated from God through the disobedience of Adam. We are reconciled back to God through the obedience of Jesus Christ. Additionally, we are saved from the wrath to come. So many people experience fear and stress about "Judgment Day," where they picture themselves before an angry God. But we have already been "judged" through Christ. His blood appeased the wrath of God's judgment of sin once and for all. We simply believe this truth and receive the benefits of the gift of righteousness which is our right standing before God. We now have peace with God and trust in the blood that forever washes away our sins. We are clean!

SOLVING THE PROBLEM OF THE SIN NATURE: THE CROSS

One summer as a child, I was assigned daily chores along with my siblings. One of my tasks was weeding the flower beds, and the youthful urge to play rather than work dominated my reasoning. I quickly lopped off the top of the weeds, producing the appearance of a pristine garden on the surface. But underneath and out of sight, hiding deep in the dark soil, the roots of the weeds were sucking the nutrients out of the earth, fortifying their stronghold while robbing the flowers of their full potential. Within the next few days, the top of the weeds grew back, and the task became more laborious. That experience brought the wisdom that if I invested the time to pull out the roots, the weeds would not proliferate and the flowers would flourish. Our hearts are much like a flower garden.

It is possible to go through life by lopping off the symptoms of stress and appearing pristine on the outside while ignoring the root of our problems. Like weeds, the deeply hidden secrets of our hearts silently rob us of the abundant life for which we were created. While our problems may seem impossible to uproot, God has already provided a solution.

It is clear the blood that Jesus shed was the complete payment for our sins. It fulfilled the requirement to redeem, reconcile and restore humankind back to the original value and relationship which our Creator has longed for ever since the fall of Adam and Eve. Because of Christ's willing sacrifice, there is no more guilt, shame or stress associated with our past sins. God dealt with the sins of his created ones, but how did he resolve the *sin nature*, the root and cause of all sins?

Initially God gave his law to Moses for the children of Israel. In part, these rules and regulations required conformity to God's justness thereby outlining his principles of conduct. This became known as the law of Moses. With the condition of humankind in their fallen nature and without their spiritual connection to God, the law of Moses defined the standard of righteous living. It was able to protect the people from the consequences of sin and provide a system of how to have a relationship with God and then one another. The problem was, nobody could keep the law. The sin nature inherited from Adam was too overpowering. Romans reveals, "What the Law could not do, because human nature was weak, God did. He condemned sin in human nature by sending his own Son, who came with a nature like our sinful nature, to do away with sin."[11]

First Corinthians says, "and the strength of sin is the law."[12] For example, we have speed limit signs and flashing signals that establish and reinforce driving laws, yet many drivers virtually ignore them and recklessly speed on by—until they spy a police officer parked on the side of the road. Suddenly, their driving behavior becomes downright civilized. They remain cautious until the officer is far out of sight in their rearview mirror and then resume their reckless driving habits. What happened? The law did not change anything; it was the *threat* of a violation that influenced temporary behavior modification so they could avoid the consequences of their wrongdoing.

There's a powerful urge to return to our old ways. I remember unexpectedly bumping into a patient from my nutrition practice at the local grocery store. Her shopping basket contained doughnuts, soda and other foods she was supposed to be avoiding. After attempting to conceal her shocked expression of *Oh, Busted!* from her face, she stammered, "Uh, um, these aren't for me, they're for my husband." Current statistics indicate that about 95 percent of all diets fail. That is true because the participants on a diet regiment are made aware of what they should and shouldn't eat. The more they focus on food, including its associated emotions, the more they seem to gravitate toward the "no-no's" and give in to the proverbial cookie jar—especially during times of stress.

When Adam had his original connection to God (his spirit life), he relied on that spiritual relationship to live. Once he lost that original connection, he became dependent on the five senses dominating his soul life instead of a vibrant spiritual relationship with God. The human soul includes the emotions, reasoning, and will of the mind. The Bible discusses *soul life* as having the potential of being influenced either by the flesh (life persuaded by the sinful nature) or by the Spirit of God. The body is subject to the soul, yet the soul, born with Adam's fallen nature, is accustomed to having the five senses run the show.

The law cannot tame the flesh but, in fact, entices the soul to defiantly perform the opposite of God's will thus causing sin and producing stress. David wrote in the Psalms: "For my sins have flooded over my head; they are a burden too heavy for me to bear."[13] Nothing could reform the "sin nature," not rules and regulations, not self-reflection and discipline, and not programs of behavior modification. The apostle Paul explained, "For when we were in the realm of the flesh, the sinful passions aroused by the law were at work in us, so that we bore fruit for death. But sin, seizing the opportunity afforded by the commandment, produced in me every kind of coveting. For apart from the law, sin was dead."[14] In this context, "flesh" refers to the fallen sinful nature of humankind, which is rebellious to the things of God. "Death" pertains to separation from God.

We were originally created in the image of God, who is Spirit, but after the loss of spirit life, all generations born from the bloodline of Adam inherited his sin nature. Genesis tells us, "And Adam lived one hundred and thirty years, and begot a son in his own likeness, after his image, and named him Seth."[15] Notice that Adam's son was in his own *likeness* and *image*, which was just body and soul. Adam's offense brought him the judgment and sentence of death. This condemnation was passed on to those born of Adam, and they received the same penalty because they inherited his sinful nature. Before Christ came, sin was the cruel taskmaster that had dominion over every human being. The only way to escape the sinful nature of Adam was to die to it. Jesus Christ's death on the cross dealt with our sin nature.

Paul's writings in Scripture provide numerous insights:[16]

"I have been crucified with Christ;"

"How shall we who died to sin live any longer in it?"

"Since we have been united with him in his death…"

"Knowing this, that our old self was crucified with Him, in order that our body of sin might be done away with, so that we would no longer be slaves to sin."

113

"Now if we died with Christ…"

"For you died…"

"I have been crucified in relation to the world, set free from the stifling atmosphere of pleasing others and fitting into the little patterns that they dictate."

"being conformed to His death…"

"Those who belong to Christ have crucified their old nature with all that it loved and lusted for."

Do you see the recurring message? The old self, the sin nature we inherited from Adam, was crucified on the cross! Jesus bore all our sins and sicknesses—including every mental anguish and emotional pain. They were nailed to the cross with him—crucified with him—and then buried with him.

In the epistle to the Colossians, Paul explained that the power of the crucifixion came "by canceling the record of debt that stood against us with its legal demands. This he set aside, nailing it to the cross."[17] This practice of canceling a debt was culturally understood by those who lived during the time Colossians was written. Individual debts were recorded on a piece of parchment paper and then nailed to the city gates and displayed for everyone to see. Sometimes a patron came along, recognized a person's debt and then paid it in full on their behalf. Once the debt was completely paid, the notice was blotted out with the paper doubled in half and nailed up on the gate so that everyone could see it was taken care of. In the same way Jesus Christ, our benefactor, took notice of all our sinful debts and blotted out the public records held against us. He permanently removed our sin-debt when he was nailed to the cross. A correlating verse concerning the coming Messiah further illustrates this Eastern custom. "Speak to the heart of Jerusalem, and cry unto her, that her time of suffering is accomplished, that her iniquity is pardoned; for she hath received of Jehovah's hand double for all her sins."[18] The term "double for all her sins" is the comforting and prophetic declaration of their debt being doubled over and completely paid for, setting them free from the burden of sin.

In his letter to the Romans, Paul declared these words: "Or do you not know that we who are baptized in Jesus Christ are baptized in his death? We are buried with him in baptism to death...For if we were planted together with him in the likeness of his death."[19] Notice the expressions, "baptized in Jesus Christ" and "baptized in his death." Through baptism in his name and in his death, we were immersed into all that he is and all that his name represents. Being planted together in his death defines an identifiable, intimate and inseparable union with Christ thereby encompassing the crucifixion, death and burial of the sin nature. It wasn't that the soul was put to death, but rather the "old nature" that operated through the soul.

The soul of a person is also referred to as the breath of God and the spirit of humankind. That spirit was never designed to function separately from the Spirit of God. In its state of separation from God, which is the nature of Adam, the human spirit is influenced by the five senses and naturally does its own thing. With the death penalty of Adam being paid by Jesus Christ, the human spirit once again has access to the power that comes from dependence on the Spirit of God. This enables us to be free from the self-natured influence over of our soul life and to unify our spirits with God's Spirit, thus fulfilling God's will and purpose for our lives.

Our sins were dealt with once and for all by the sacrificial blood of Jesus Christ. Our sin nature was vanquished when he went to the cross, was crucified, died and was buried. Even the act of the Lord's burial is important: with the final act of our being laid in the grave, *our* lives and relationships were separated from the old, worldly ways of doing things. This included the inherited old nature of Adam and our identification of being slaves to sin.

It is at this point that a phenomenal transition occurs—one where we discover we have so much more than Adam, Jacob, David, Asaph, or Jehoshaphat ever had; that is, the reality of a new life.

References:

1.   2 Corinthians 4:4

2.   Leviticus 17:11

3.   Hebrews 10:2-3 and 11-12 (TLB)

4.   Romans 3:24-25 (ESV)

5.   Ephesians 1:7 (GNT)

6.   1 John 1:7 (WT)

7.   1 Peter 1:18-19 (VOICE)

8.   Ephesians 2:13 (MSG)

9.   Revelation 12:10

10.   Romans 5:8-10 (ESV)

11.   Romans 8:3 (GNT)

12.   1 Corinthians 15:56

13.   Psalm 38:4 (HCSB)

14.   Romans 7:5, 8 (NIV)

15.   Genesis 5:3

16.   Galatians 2:20a; Romans 6:2b; Romans 6:5a (NLT); Romans 6:6 (NAS); Romans 6:8a; Colossians 3:3a; Galatians 6:14b (MSG); Philippians 3:10b and Galatians 5:24 (J.B.PHILLIPS)

17.   Colossians 2:14 (ESV)

18.   Isaiah 40:2 (DBY)

19.   Romans 6:3, 4a, 5a (APNT)

CHAPTER 10

A NEW LIFE - A NEW NATURE - A NEW NAME

G od did not leave his Son in the grave, but raised him up to life. When he was raised, we were raised with him. Just as we were identified with Christ in the likeness of his death, we shall be "united with him in a resurrection like his."[1]

Jesus exchanged his life for ours. He died so that we could be made alive! "And you [He made alive when you] were [spiritually] dead and separated from Him because of your transgressions and sins."[2] We did not make ourselves alive. No works of our flesh brought about this righteous act. Colossians affirms, "You were dead because of your sins and because your sinful nature was not yet cut away. Then God made you alive with Christ, for he forgave all our sins."[3]

What caused this marvelous miracle to take place? "But God still loved us with such great love. He is so rich in compassion and mercy. Even when we were dead and doomed in our many sins, he united us into the very life of Christ and saved us by his wonderful grace! He raised us up with Christ the exalted One, and we ascended with him into the glorious perfection and authority of the heavenly realm, for we are now co-seated as one with Christ!"[4] It was because of God's love and grace that he took us from death (meaning separation from him) and raised us to a new life. As a result, "anyone who belongs to Christ has become a new person. The old life is gone;

a new life has begun!"[5] The Weymouth Translation renders it, "The old state of things has passed away."

BORN OF THE SPIRIT: ETERNAL LIFE

The first epistle of Peter declares, "For Christ also died for sins once for all, the righteous for the unrighteous, that he might bring us to God, being put to death in the flesh but made alive in the spirit;"[6] This verse reveals another benefit pertaining to the death and resurrection of Christ. It's found in the phrase, "bring us to God." Picture this: just as a newborn baby is presented to its mother and father at birth, Jesus presents us as newly "born again" ones to our heavenly Father. Being born again introduces us into the most tender loving relationship in all creation. We become endowed with new rights and privileges as sons and daughters of God. (The word translated "bring" in this passage is also translated in the noun form as *access*. We will discover more about this access later.)

John's gospel tells us the story of a religious leader named Nicodemus, who once had an interesting conversation with Jesus Christ. The Messiah informed him, "Most assuredly, I say to you, unless one is born again, he cannot see the kingdom of God...That which is born of the flesh is flesh; and that which is born of the Spirit is spirit."[7] Do you remember one of the points from chapter nine, that we were born of the flesh into the lineage of Adam, having just body and soul? When we are born *again*, we receive that spirit life, which is eternal: "As persons who have been born again, not from fallible seed, but that which is infallible, by the living word of God which stands for eternity."[8]

Just what are we to do with this new life? We continually and enthusiastically pursue the things of God! "Since you have been raised to new life with Christ, set your sights on the realities of heaven, where Christ sits in the place of honor at God's right hand." Because we are united and risen with Christ, our newly appointed position is at the right hand of God. We now have authority in Christ and access to the throne of grace. Even more, "He has rescued us from the dominion of darkness and brought us into the kingdom of the Son he loves,"[9] We are citizens in the kingdom of God; the rules of his kingdom are not the same as those of the world. When I travel to different countries, nearly everything around me changes: culture, laws, protocols and manners, even currency. I won't get very far trying to spend pesos in India or rupees in Mexico. In the kingdom of God the currency consists of love, prosperity, health, joy, peace and goodness. The currency of this world includes negativity, sickness, poverty, strife, and evil—none of which are accepted by the bank of heaven.

> *Eternal life does not begin when we go to heaven; it commences the very moment we confess Jesus as Lord and believe God raised him from the dead.*

Additionally, even though we are newcomers, we are not outcasts or strangers in this new kingdom. "Look with wonder at the depth of the Father's marvelous love that he has lavished on us! He has called us and made us his very own beloved children . . . Beloved, we are God's children right now."[10] We have a new life because of the accomplishments of Christ, *and* this life is an eternal one. "And this is the testimony, that God gave us eternal life, and this life is in his Son. Whoever has the Son has life; whoever does not have the Son of God does not have life."[11] We are going to live forever! John's gospel develops this further: "Now this is eternal life, that they will know you, that you alone are the God of truth and he whom you have sent [is] Jesus the Messiah."[12] Eternal life does not begin when we go to heaven; it commences the very moment we confess Jesus as Lord and believe God raised him from the dead.

He is our heavenly Father. He's not some distant relative known for rare visits. He knows us so intimately that he even knows the number of hairs on our head. This knowing is experiential, not just an acknowledgement of someone. It pertains to a personal and intimate relationship with the only true God and Jesus Christ his Son. I'm familiar with the teller at the bank or the cashier at the supermarket by casual acquaintance, but I *know* my wife, friends, and colleagues through frequent and personally shared experiences with them. Relationships are initiated and fostered by spending time together and developing trust. The greater the relationship we desire, the more time we will devote to those with whom we enter into relationship.

This new life we have is spirit life. What Adam lost has been restored to us. The book of Titus tells us, "He saved us not by works of righteousness that we have done but on the basis of his mercy, through the washing of the new birth and the renewing of the Holy Spirit."[13] We have been completely cleansed and the spiritual connection has been restored through receiving the Holy Spirit. The Bible offers several expressions of the Holy Spirit. The identity and work of the Holy Spirit includes: the Spirit of truth, the Comforter, Christ in you, the new man, the new nature, the new creation, the inner man, the inward man, and other characteristics and attributes.

Paul emphasized the contrast between the old life and the new in his letter to the Romans.

"Could it be any clearer? Our old way of life was nailed to the cross with Christ, a decisive end to that sin-miserable life—no longer at sin's every beck and call! What we believe is this: If we get included in Christ's sin-conquering death, we also get included in his life-saving resurrection. We know that when Jesus was raised from the dead it was a signal of the end of death-as-the-end. Never again will death have the last word. When Jesus died, he took sin down with him, but alive he brings God down to us. From now on, think of it this way: Sin speaks a dead language that means nothing to you; God speaks your mother tongue, and you hang on every word. You are dead to sin and alive to God. That's what Jesus did. That means you must not give sin a vote in the way you conduct your lives. Don't give it the time of day. Don't even run little errands that are connected with that old way of life. Throw yourselves wholeheartedly and full-time—remember, you've been raised from the dead!—into God's way of doing things. Sin can't tell you how to live. After all, you're not living under that old tyranny any longer. You're living in the freedom of God. So, since we're out from under the old tyranny, does that mean we can live any old way we want? Since we're free in the freedom of God, can we do anything that comes to mind? Hardly. You know well enough from your own experience that there are some acts of so-called freedom that destroy freedom. Offer yourselves to sin, for instance, and it's your last free act. But offer yourselves to the ways of God and the freedom never quits. All your lives you've let sin tell you what to do. But thank God you've started listening to a new master, one whose commands set you free to live openly in his freedom!"[14]

This passage reveals four imperatives for believers in Christ to practice:

1. Consider ourselves to be dead to sin in the same way Christ died once and for all to sin.

2. Consider ourselves alive to God through Christ Jesus, just as Christ lives for him.

3. Do not let sin reign in our lives to obey its passionate lusts.

4. Decisively present, offer, and yield ourselves (our bodies and souls, including our talents, gifts, and abilities) as righteous instruments to God.

Many people, including those who are born again, believe they are free to do whatever they want, but Paul clearly wrote in his letter that we are actually servants to the one we are obeying. We determine whether we are going to have a life of separation from God, walking by the flesh and serving sin—or the new life, through Christ, of serving a righteous God.

Several of Paul's letters contain additional exhortations to the believers, "to put off your old self, which belongs to your former manner of life and is corrupt through deceitful desires, and to be renewed in the spirit of your minds, and to put on the new self, created after the likeness of God in true righteousness and holiness."[15] In this context, "manner of life" refers to the behavior or habits of the old nature. To be "renewed in the spirit of your mind" is a continuous action where the life of the individual is refreshed with characteristics that are new in quality because they have not been experienced before. A similar concept is found in Romans: "Therefore, I beg you, my brothers, by the mercies of God, to present your bodies a living and holy and acceptable sacrifice to God in reasonable service. And do not imitate this world, but be turned the other way by the renewal of your minds and distinguish what is the good and acceptable and perfect will of God."[16] Think about these exhortations: *Put off, be renewed, put on, present.* Colossians offers more along the same line. "You're done with that old life. It's like a filthy set of ill-fitting clothes you've stripped off and put in the fire. Now you're dressed in a new wardrobe. Every item of your new way of life is custom-made by the Creator, with his label on it. All the old fashions are now obsolete."[17]

When my twin daughters were young children, they loved to play in our backyard. One day it began to rain lightly, but that did not deter them from staying outdoors. Eventually they decided to come into the house, but my wife and I intercepted them because they were covered with mud, including their clothes, hair and shoes. They looked so cute with their bright blue eyes happily peering through their grubby little faces, but we firmly told them, "Take all your clothes off so you don't track your dirty stuff into the house." We were tempted to march them back outside and hose them down, but instead we carried them to the shower, cleaned them up, and put warm fresh clothes on their squeaky-clean bodies. In the same manner, children of God simply put off the old nature (Adam) and put on the new (Christ). "And all who have been united with Christ in baptism have put on Christ, like putting on new clothes."[18] Putting on the new nature is being clothed once again with that glorious image with which God created humankind in the beginning. We are also restored to the dignity of children of God. "And if children, then heirs—heirs of God and fellow heirs with Christ."[19] Believers in Christ are no longer identified by what they do, but by who they are: sons and daughters of God!

Our inheritance includes the right to use the name of Jesus Christ. When we use his name, we exercise and represent his authority in our everyday lives. Shortly after my children got their driver's licenses, they were eager to run errands, especially to go get take-out food. I simply handed them the keys to the car and gave them my credit card to cover the purchase. Whatever resources were linked to my name on the credit card empowered the girls to act on my behalf and get the same result as if I was personally present. The name of Jesus Christ has the very resources of heaven behind the name, empowering us to act on his behalf and get the same results as if he were personally present. We now have the authority and privilege to pray in his name, to heal sickness and disease in his name and to cast out devils in his name. Using his name to overcome stress in our lives and the lives of others is a major benefit of the new life we have in Christ.

With this new nature of Christ in us, we are empowered to act in his place. We are Jesus Christ to the world. "So we are Christ's ambassadors; God is making his appeal through us. We speak for Christ when we plead, 'Come back to God!'"[20] When we learn these vibrant truths, this gospel of grace, we are excited to walk out in our new identity and explore who we are in Christ.

123

Venturing out on this journey brings an exhilarating feeling of new found freedom. It is truly a breath of fresh air! Soon, however, we discover conflict arising and producing unexpected frustration and stress. This conflict is really between the old nature and the new. The next chapter will discuss why that conflict exists and how to escape the old nature and live in the new one.

References

1.   Romans 6:5b (ESV)
2.   Ephesians 2:1 (AMP)
3.   Colossians 2:13 (NLT)
4.   Ephesians 2:4-6 (TPT)
5.   2 Corinthians 5:17 (NLT, WEY)
6.   1 Peter 3:18 (RSV)
7.   John 3:3b, 6
8.   1 Peter 1:23 (ABPE)
9.   Colossians 3:1 (NLT), from Ephesians 2:6,18 and Colossians 1:13 (NIV)
10.   1 John 3:1a, 2a (TPT)
11.   1 John 5:11-12 (ESV)
12.   John 17:3 (APNT)
13.   Titus 3:5 (NET)
14.   Romans 6:6-18 (MSG)
15.   Ephesians 4:22-24 (ESV)
16.   Romans 12:1-2 (APNT)
17.   Colossians 3:9b, 10 (MSG)
18.   Galatians 3:27 (NLT)
19.   Romans 8:17a (ESV)
20.   2 Corinthians 5:20 (NLT)

CHAPTER 11

RELEASE FROM THE OLD NATURE

When we first enter this new life, we typically begin our journey as believers by walking in the new nature with an enthusiastic devotion. Soon, however, we realize there are still areas where we struggle and remain in the clutches of the old nature. Certain sinful habits continue flaunting themselves by intimidating us and imposing their apparent dominance over our lives. This deceptive illusion causes us to doubt the reality of the new birth. Whether they are self-imposed or subtly suggested by others, the demands to perform, reform and conform relentlessly increase our stress levels. We wonder what happened to our acknowledgment of the blood of Jesus Christ, the crucifixion of the old nature and our new nature of righteousness.

Feelings of guilt, shame and condemnation sweep over our souls as the devil attacks with slanderous words of accusation, reminding us of our weaknesses and influencing our minds to plummet back into sin consciousness. We begin to think, *I need to escape this enslavement. Perhaps there are still some sins I forgot to confess. Maybe repenting of them by changing my behavior and resolving to never do them again will please God. Then I might find more favor with him.* As we try to overcome the struggle in our own strength, a repugnant taste of defeat intensifies. Every effort to measure up to God's expectations seems useless. We discover it is one thing to acknowledge our new life in Christ, but another thing to practice it.

LEGALISM VERSUS LIBERTY

Why do many fall into this no-win cycle? It is the conflict between religion and relationship most every believer faces. Remember, God gave his commandments to Moses as written in the Torah. These laws communicated God's righteous standards and provided guidelines of conduct for Old Testament believers. Religious leaders, however, distorted these precepts by mingling their own traditions with God's laws. These deviations ultimately forged an imitation of holiness known as *legalism*.

Legalism is a false religion that has the appearance of holiness but actually stems from self-righteousness and devilish pride. It is a "holier than thou" attitude. The requirements of legalism demand one must approach God through the gateway of the approval and acceptance of others. It incorporates the traditions of rituals, rites, rules and regulations to obtain God's favor, blessings and love. Legalism is authoritative, controlling and manipulative. Its *modus operandi* is behavior modification through fear, oppression, guilt and shame. It insists that one's vocabulary, beliefs and methodologies conform to its apparently neat and tidy definitions. Legalism breeds superficial performance while imposing a duty of obligation. It promotes doing all the right things for all the wrong reasons. (God's grace, on the other hand, inspires and nurtures a genuinely deep and loving response to his kind benevolence and infinite goodness.) Legalists implement unconditional compliance with their list of "do's and don'ts." They historically hide within gatherings of God's people and hunt for unsuspecting victims. Once they find their prey, they attempt to bring well-meaning believers under a yoke of bondage.

What makes legalism so attractive? It is the innate hunger to be right. The appearance of righteousness provides false feelings of comfort and security. Why? Because appearing to be right appeals to the approval of others. When an individual, group, organization or culture claims to be right, the scheme of helping others to "become right" resides beneath the surface. The enticement of their approval hinges upon adopting their mandated approach to pleasing God. Consider the marked difference between what many declare to be right and what is indeed true. Legalism promises the strength of unity but thrives on classifications, levels of distinction and hierarchies. Failure to align with other's expectations results in rejection.

Before the birth of Christ, a group of legalistic leaders called Pharisees had emerged in Israel. They positioned themselves so that the public would consider them the righteously elite. Their external performance was polished by a display of outward dedication in keeping the law of Moses. While they themselves could not fulfill their own burdensome requirements, they imposed unattainable ordinances on others. Jesus exposed their religious system and called them hypocrites. Do legalists still exist today? Absolutely! Here are two examples.

I have a friend who lives in a rural, so-called religious community. There is such a pervasive fear of being judged and condemned that some people travel to another county to take in a movie because movie-going is not accepted by others in their own community. A family decided to escape these legalistic impositions and withdrew from participating in many religious activities. One day there was a tragic accident and a few members of this family were killed. At the funeral service, an elder stood up and proclaimed, "This is God's judgment on those who do not abide by our rules of faith and practice." (Since then, many in the community have decided to seek God's help and be liberated from this tyrannical oppression.)

What makes legalism so attractive? It is the innate hunger to be right. The appearance of righteousness provides false feelings of comfort and security.

While traveling to other parts of the globe, I was introduced to a variety of cultures. Another eye-opening experience took place when I was invited by the former president of a major denomination to attend a Sunday church service with him. He proudly announced that over 6,000 people showed up one half-hour early just to get a seat. Having had previous exposure to this denomination in other countries, I assumed and anticipated a lively event of singing, clapping, dancing and other expressions of praise to God. But it was just the opposite. I was puzzled as I scanned the immense congregation and saw an endless sea of unhappiness. After the service I inquired as to why this gathering was lifeless. The reply startled me as my host explained. "A long time ago, missionaries came from another country. They brought resources to build this church, but with those resources came the requirement to adopt their way of doing things including the integration of their traditions and culture." When I asked why people didn't leave and go elsewhere, the response came in a parable. "If you tie a baby elephant to a stake with a metal chain around its leg and if it attempts to break loose, its tender skin will be gashed and it will feel intense pain. The consequence will remain so vivid in the elephant's memory, that as it becomes older, you can tie a thread around its leg and it won't try to escape. If our young and tenderhearted people try leaving the church or resisting our ways, we inflict pain by publicly rebuking and embarrassing them so that they will not consider repeating this error."

An inward change of the heart is not achieved through what we attempt to do in our own strength. Genuine transformation is determined through believing in what has already been accomplished for us in Christ.

Religious legalism offers endless remedies to reform the old nature, but these works-based methodologies only further develop self-righteousness and hinder God's favor. These suggested solutions include rules and regulations of what we must do or not do in order to improve our standing with God. They also fabricate measurements of righteousness whereby we may compare our performance to others. While compliance with these demands addresses the outward appearance of behavior modification, it simply polishes the veneer of pretense. Hypocritical intentions allow the habits of the old nature to coexist under the guise of the new. An inward change of the heart is not achieved through what we attempt to do in our own strength. Genuine transformation is determined through believing in what has already been accomplished for us in Christ. This includes a righteous standing before God. The church epistles in the New Testament are dedicated to instructing born again believers about their new life in Christ. However, if we try to discern these realities without God's helpful insight, we may interpret the Scriptures through a legalistic lens and turn encouraging exhortations into demanding dictates.

Certain commitments and decisions may assume an outward form of holiness, but they are fruitless endeavors if they did not originate with God. These sincere intentions may include praying, Bible study, attending meetings, participating in programs, volunteering, renewing one's faith, vowing fresh resolutions and other disciplines. Increasing the frequency and intensity of these activities without God's direction only results in frustrating his grace from flowing into our lives.

This is not something new. The epistle to the Colossians addressed these same concerns. "For you were included in the death of Christ and have died with him to the religious system and powers of this world. Don't retreat back to being bullied by the standards and opinions of religion—for example, their strict requirements, 'You can't associate with that person!' or, 'Don't eat that!' or, 'You can't touch that!' These are the doctrines of men and corrupt customs that are worthless to help you spiritually. For though they may appear to possess the promise of wisdom in their submission to God through the deprivation of their physical bodies, it is actually nothing more than empty rules rooted in religious rituals!"[1]

129

Under no circumstances should our works be performed with the intention of gaining God's acceptance. We are already accepted by God through our new life in Christ and his accomplished works of righteousness. Religion always tries to control the flesh through rigid edicts. A person cannot produce godly fruit by planting and cultivating the seeds of ungodly principles.

Religious leaders during Jesus' earthly ministry were blind to his redemptive purposes. The reason was that they were consumed with their self-righteous works of fulfilling the law of Moses. Paul, an apostle of Jesus Christ, was previously one of those religious leaders. He, too, was a Pharisee and sat at the feet of Gamaliel, a reputable doctor of the law. This mode of learning was administered through a combination of demonstration and disciplined instruction.

In his letter to the Philippians, Paul communicated that he was blameless concerning the righteousness which is in the law, meaning that as a Pharisee, he met every requirement the law placed upon him. His outward appearance seemed impeccable, yet, as he admitted, the law exposed his sin of inordinate desires.[2] After a remarkable encounter with the resurrected Christ, Paul was born again. Later he wrote the aforementioned "church epistles" to the believers of the first-century church. This church was not some new religion, denomination or organization. It was called the body of Christ, a living organism made up of "whoevers" that believed in the resurrected Christ and recognized him as the head of the church.

Paul preached about the relationship of the law of Moses to the believer. He explained that they were released from the law. What does "released" mean? Suppose you were chosen for jury duty, and the night before you were to appear at the courthouse you received a call informing you that you had been *released* from your obligation. Would you still report to court the next morning? Of course not. You are excused from any further requirements. Likewise, believers are dead to the law. But don't misunderstand. It was not that the law itself was wrong or even evil. Its purpose was good in that it exposed the sin nature. However, the law did not comprise the grace or power to change the heart.

Think of it this way. Suppose your car starts making a strange noise and you are not sure what's going on with it. You would probably take it to a mechanic who hooks it up to a computer to run a diagnostic test on the vehicle. When it reveals what's wrong with the car, you don't conclude the test was evil because it exposed the problem. Rather, it was helpful in identifying the cause of the trouble. In the same way, the law helped expose the problem of the old sin nature, but the law could not remedy it. Paul wrote regarding the law. "It is impossible to do what God's standards demand because of the weakness our human nature has."[3] He went on to exclaim,

"I just don't get it, for I am not practicing what I want to do, but instead, I keep on doing what I hate doing. And because I do the very thing I don't desire to do, I am acknowledging and agreeing that my behavior is wrong and confirming that the law's righteous standards are good. But it is no longer me doing it, but the sin dwelling in me. I realize that no good thing dwells in my unspiritual self, that is in the old nature. The desire to do good is present, but to actually perform it, I don't know how to carry it out. If I practice that which I don't want to do, it is no longer I producing it but rather the sin dwelling in my old nature. Because evil is right there with the desire to do good, I discover the law; but not after Moses, for I have been delivered from that, but from a newly discovered law after the inner man, the new nature, the newness of the Spirit. I delight in this newly found law of God; however, I see a different law in the members of my body associated with the old nature, warring against the newly discovered law in my mind, and bringing me into captivity of the law of sin and death that engages the members of my body associated with the old nature."[4]

Perhaps you, too, have experienced this conflict. Paul exposed this internal hostility when he wrote, "For everything the flesh desires goes against the Spirit, and everything the Spirit desires goes against the flesh. There is a constant battle raging between them that prevents you from doing the good you want to do."[5] The new nature of the Spirit and the old nature of the flesh are contrary to each another. Even though the old nature that resided in our hearts and souls was crucified with Christ, its habits still linger as impressions in the memory of our minds.

When Moses led the children of Israel from their slavery in Egypt to the land of promise, they were at first exhilarated with joy and sang praises to God. But they soon complained about what they were going to eat and drink and their jubilance eroded into ungratefulness. They even contemplated returning to their old lives of harsh and bitter bondage. Their lack of trust in God became evident as their unbelief embraced "the good old days" back in Egypt, which in reality were anything but good. Their slave mentality inhibited them from moving toward their new promised land. Many of them wanted to return to Egypt!

It reminds me of the time my family had a beautiful border collie who was a part of our everyday life for fourteen years. His name was Cricket (named after the sport, not the insect). He loved to greet people at the door. He playfully brought a ball or toy to instigate a throw and fetch routine and looked forward to his twice-a-day walks. Cricket enjoyed life as a dog. Yet when he passed away, my family did not have a taxidermist preserve his body, nor did we keep his scheduled veterinarian appointments. We did not renew his dog license, and we stopped collecting coupons for pet food and supplies. Fond memories of Cricket occasionally pop up. Every so often we hear what sounds like a familiar bark. Other times we may notice a blanket in a dimly lit room and mistakenly envision him quietly lying on the floor. But he's gone and therefore we don't dwell on the intermittent and fading reminders of his existence.

Or consider another analogy from history, during the time of the U.S. Civil War. Even though President Abraham Lincoln legally abolished slavery and declared freedom throughout the land, many slaves continued to work the fields and serve their masters as though nothing had really changed. Ignorance and apprehension of their proclaimed freedom crippled them from boldly living a life of liberty. In the same way Jesus Christ paid the price for the believers' liberty, yet so many are still ignorant and apprehensive of their freedom from sin and their rights and privileges as sons and daughters of God. They continue serving the master of the sin nature and even worse, like the Israelites, consider returning to their old ways instead of walking into their promised place of a new life.

If our old nature was crucified with Christ, why does it still seem to reign? What keeps us from releasing it as we should? Experts in child psychology and early childhood development have published their observations of a period of life called the "formative years." Their research suggests that the foundation of our attitudes, belief systems, philosophies, prejudices, stereotypes, habit patterns and behavioral instincts are well developed by the time we are five years old. Our parental and familial surroundings often provide a fertile breeding ground that determines our life-long perceptions. Our hearts continue being impressionable and pliable until we reach approximately ten years of age, when logic, reasoning and judgment are further established and woven into our thinking processes. This means that we enter adolescence and later, adulthood, with these youthful traits integrated within our souls. Likewise, any ungodly impressions shaping our character may develop into strongholds of tradition unless they are challenged by spiritual truths from God. (Do you remember how we previously learned from the prophet Isaiah that worldly traditions render God's word ineffective? It's the same with our life experience and perceptions.)

Before coming to Christ, all of us "whoevers" were sinners. But those who believe on him are now made righteous by his blood.

Subsequently, after the old nature is crucified with Christ, the life of the resurrected Christ comes to live in our hearts as the new nature through the Holy Spirit. Jesus promised, if we believe on him, we can do the same and greater works than he did. Then what is the obstacle holding us back? Is this new life in Christ unattainable? Should believers throw their hands up and cry, "What's the use?" Paul the apostle felt this very same frustration. He bemoaned, "I am a miserable man! Who will rescue me from this body of death?" Like us, Paul needed to be rescued from the stress of the old nature. When Paul penned this plea, he may have been articulating his analogy to a form of capital punishment carried out during that time. A decaying corpse was tied face-to-face to the person sentenced to execution! The stench of the dead body invariably extinguished the life of the condemned person. Paul vividly communicated this picture of the life of the believer, clothed in the new nature, still being bound to the death of the old nature.

What did Paul do to resolve his dilemma? He cried to God for help when he was afflicted by stress. Paul then shared the glorious answer he was given: "In my mind I am God's willing servant, but in my own nature I am bound fast, as I say, to the law of sin and death. It is an agonizing situation, and who on earth can set me free from the clutches of my sinful nature? I thank God there is a way out through Jesus Christ our Lord." The Living Bible puts it in the past tense, "Thank God! It has been done by Jesus Christ our Lord. He has set me free."[6] Paul is discussing two laws: the law of God and the law of sin. The law of God is the same as the law of the inner man, the new nature as described in Romans 7:21-22. It is also called "the law of the Spirit of life in Christ Jesus" and "the perfect law of liberty." *The law of sin* refers to the law of Moses, which exposes, excites, and produces sins in the flesh, that is, the old nature. It is also called the law of sin and death.[7]

In Romans chapter 7 Paul concluded that he served the law of God with his mind, but served the law of sin from his old nature, which though dead, still activated thoughts to entice a return to the life he led before coming to Christ. God promised, "I will put my law in their inward parts, and write it in their hearts; and will be their God, and they shall be my people."[8] This law was introduced with the coming of the New Testament. This new law of God, the "law of the Spirit of life in Christ Jesus," is superior to the law of Moses. While the law of Moses activates the old sin nature, this new law of God strengthens the heart and mind to respond to the desires of God and gives the grace to fulfill those desires. This is the release from the law.

Now we will explore how this greater law of the Spirit of life in Christ Jesus transforms us into living victoriously.

References

1. Colossians 2:20-23 (TPT)

2. Philippians 3:6, Romans 7:7 and 8

3. Romans 8:3a (GW)

4. Paraphrase from Romans 7:15-23

5. Galatians 5:17 (RSV)

6. Romans 7:24-25 (J.B. PHILLIPS) and verse 25 (TLB)

7. Romans 8:2 and James 1:25

8. Jeremiah 31:33b (KJV)

CHAPTER 12

THE JOURNEY TO VICTORIOUS LIVING

Think of a caterpillar. It is subject to the law of gravity until it is changed into a beautiful butterfly. Then the law of aerodynamics supersedes the law of gravity and it takes off graciously into the new journey of a transformed life. The butterfly is designed to fly. It would be ludicrous and unnatural for it to continue to crawl on the ground as it once did as a caterpillar. The believer in Christ is designed to graciously take off and live by the Spirit. It is just as ludicrous and unnatural for us to continue to walk in the old nature as we once did as unbelievers. Why would anyone want to continue to live by the old nature when this new life is available?

God is Spirit and his very nature is love; in fact, it is impossible for him *not* to love. The new law of God is the spiritual law of love. The Scriptures illuminate this truth: "Let no debt remain outstanding, except the continuing debt to love one another, for whoever loves others has fulfilled the law ... Love does no harm to a neighbor. Therefore love is the fulfillment of the law ... For the entire law is fulfilled in keeping this one command: 'Love your neighbor as yourself.' ... If you really keep the royal law found in Scripture, 'Love your neighbor as yourself,' you are doing right." Love never ends, fails or falls short.[1]

This law of love is fulfilled in walking by the Spirit. If you are led by the Spirit, you are not under the law. To be led by the Spirit is to be led by love! If we are walking in love, we don't need laws such as, "Do not steal, do not commit adultery, do not tell lies about others" as found in the Ten Commandments. Why? Because the law of *love* is greater, it supersedes the law of Moses. If we truly love, we simply won't continue walk in the old nature. It will become natural for us to walk in the new nature.

Paul revealed the key to overcoming the old nature: "Walk by the Spirit, and you will not gratify the desires of the flesh." How do we know we are walking by the Spirit? Our lives will begin bearing the fruit of the Spirit: "But the spiritual nature produces love, joy, peace, patience, kindness, goodness, faithfulness, gentleness, and self-control. There are no laws against things like that." All fruit is produced after its kind. The nature within the seed itself determines the kind of fruit it will produce. We have been born again of incorruptible seed. This incorruptible seed, Christ in us, will naturally produce the fruit of the Spirit. We have been planted with Christ and now we let his life flourish on the inside and blossom on the outside. In his letter to the Galatians, Paul wrote, "I have been crucified with Christ: and I myself no longer live, but Christ lives in me. And the real life I now have within this body is a result of my trusting in the Son of God, who loved me and gave himself for me." How could Paul say, "I myself no longer live, but Christ lives in me?" He not only considered his old nature dead, but yielded his physical and soul life to God, allowing the new nature to live through him by the Holy Spirit. Paul was walking in the same truth Jesus taught earlier. "Whoever comes after me, let them deny themselves and daily pick up their cross and follow me." This biblical idiom means to make the decision to carry out the will of another. It is a day-to-day and moment-by-moment decision.[2]

Only we can yield to Jesus as Lord each day and every moment. As we do, our new nature begins to emerge and dominate our logic and reasoning. New heavenly perspectives replace the former thought patterns ingrained in our hearts before coming to Christ. We are not only saved from sin; we are saved from ourselves. God's redemption includes being purchased and freed from the slavery of sin. Once we realize that we have been bought with the life of Jesus Christ, we begin to understand our value. We become peaceful as we rest in the assurance that God will take excellent care of his property—us!

THE RENEWED MIND

The mind of the believer is *not* automatically changed when born again. Before we were saved, our thoughts were primarily focused on the things of the flesh, the old nature. But after receiving the Holy Spirit, we as believers have the liberty to think according to the Spirit. This freedom was not available before coming to Christ. Now every Spirit-filled believer may decide whether to think and act according to the flesh or the Spirit, the old nature or the new. Thinking by the old nature is death, meaning separation from God through sin, whereas thinking spiritually with the new nature is life and peace. The old nature thinking is hostility against God because it does not submit to his higher ways and actually rebels against Christ in the believer; that is its nature. Those walking in the old nature cannot please God.[3]

We let his life flourish on the inside and blossom on the outside.

While we as believers may count the old nature as good as dead, our minds still need to be dealt with. It is not enough to painstakingly remove all the stimulating triggers of the sinful behavior from our environments. It is imperative to understand that we are engaged in a spiritual competition. The old master wants us back as slaves. The law of sin and death tries to regain its unauthorized power by trespassing on God's redeemed property, the believers. Even though we are born again, we still have the freedom to direct our lives: to choose those areas of our lives where we serve the old nature or those we submit to the new nature and lordship of Jesus Christ.

Paul tenderly writes to the believers in Rome, declaring, "Therefore, dear brothers and sisters, you have no obligation to do what your sinful nature urges you to do."[4] I once heard a minister preach on this topic. He used the illustration of a stray cat coming to someone's home looking for something to eat. Its sharp and relentless "meows" enticed the person to open the door and feed the cat hoping to silence its persistent and nerve-wracking cries. Soon the person realized this was only a temporary remedy as the cat returned the next day to repeat the ritual. As long as the person continued to cater to the cat, the relationship with it became more difficult to end. Only when the individual decided to ignore the cat's habitual whines and no longer make provision for its demands did the routine lose its tenacious grip: the cat went away. It is reminiscent of what Paul wrote in Romans, "Rather, clothe yourselves with the Lord Jesus Christ, and do not think about how to gratify the desires of the flesh."[5] Old habitual and instinctual practices will fade and finally vanish as we choose to dwell on thoughts pertaining to the new nature. This includes focusing on the more abundant life that Jesus came to make available.

Our minds are the arena of this transformation. Paul addressed this topic. "Therefore I exhort you, brothers and sisters, by the mercies of God, to present your bodies as a sacrifice—alive, holy, and pleasing to God—which is your reasonable service. Do not be conformed to this present world, but be transformed by the renewing of your mind, so that you may test and approve what is the will of God—what is good and well-pleasing and perfect."[6] This "reasonable service" is referring to the new nature, walking by the Spirit. Under the law of Moses, dead sacrifices were offered, but now we are to offer ourselves as *living* sacrifices to God. Those areas where we are hesitant to yield to the lordship of Jesus Christ and present ourselves as living sacrifices to God are the same areas where the old nature will continue to rear its ugly head. This causes bondage in our lives. So the keys to a victorious life are reckoning our old nature dead while presenting our new nature in Christ unto God as a living sacrifice through walking by the Spirit. Paul wrote these two encouraging verses that are worthy of our consideration, "For as many as are led by the Spirit of God, these are children of God," and "Now the Lord is the Spirit and where the Spirit of the Lord is, there is liberty."[7] We now determine whether or not this freedom is worth fighting for!

Paul told the believers in Corinth, "For the weapons of our warfare are not human weapons, but are made powerful by God for tearing down strongholds. We tear down arguments and every arrogant obstacle that is raised up against the knowledge of God, and we take every thought captive to make it obey Christ." The Aramaic Peshitta New Testament offers this rendering: "For the equipment of our service is not of the flesh, but of the power of God and by it, we overcome rebellious strongholds. And we pull down reasonings and all pride that elevates [itself] against the knowledge of God and we lead captive all thoughts to the obedience of Christ."[8] Strongholds are like intimidating citadels that arrogantly defy anyone to approach them. We are not to attempt to deal with them through our own abilities, but through God's powerful resources.

Responding to this exhortation allows us to see the truth and reality that God indeed works in those who walk by the Spirit. Paul's letter to the Philippians says, "For God is working in you, giving you the desire and the power to do what pleases him."[9] The words "working," "giving," and "to do" are all in the continuous present tense. God *is* constantly and presently energizing us, providing us all the resources to achieve his desires for our lives. Our response to his purpose brings him great pleasure! So then, what is our purpose? It is to seek and find *God's purpose* for our lives. He is the reason we exist! He is where our true destiny lies, and his ways are only navigable through the Lord Jesus Christ. Our lives are hid in Christ. That is why he is *our personal* Savior.

Romans affirms this truth. "We know that all things work together for good for those who love God, who are called according to his purpose, because those whom he foreknew he also predestined to be conformed to the image of his Son, that his Son would be the firstborn among many brothers and sisters."[10] "Conformed" in this verse means *to be completely formed or fashioned into another.* As we walk in the new nature, our form changes from the nature of Adam to the nature of Christ. We are no longer to fashion ourselves after the world. Think about how the world is always scheming to introduce something "new." What was in fashion yesterday is obsolete tomorrow. The world is constantly changing in government and politics, science, education and even religion. But God is unchanging and stable throughout all time. He has "no variation or shadow of turning."[11] When this analogy was first written, the stars and planets were considered to be wanderers of the night skies. Their light was observed to fluctuate, casting shadows as they rotated and orbited throughout the universe. God is a faithful constant and may be relied upon every moment. He does not change with the times; his truth endures throughout the years, spanning every generation, race and culture.

As we are transformed by the renewing of the mind, the thoughts of Christ begin to dominate the thinking patterns of our brains.

The renewing of the mind refreshes the soul with thoughts that are from God. It is a new way of thinking that exhibits a complete turnaround for the better. The renewed mind is the caterpillar changed into a butterfly. As Paul's first letter to the Corinthians inquires, "'Who can know the Lord's thoughts? Who knows enough to teach him?' But we understand these things, for we have the mind of Christ." His letter to the Philippians concurs, "You must have the same attitude that Christ Jesus had."[12] As we are transformed by the renewing of the mind, the thoughts of Christ begin to dominate the thinking patterns of our brains.

Perhaps you have heard this much quoted passage from Isaiah: "But those who wait for the Lord's help find renewed strength; they rise up as if they had eagles' wings, they run without growing weary, they walk without getting tired."[13] According to folklore, there is a certain kind of eagle throughout Asia that builds its nest high over the water. Periodically, it dives into the water at a high speed, and the impact loosens any dirty old feathers. The eagle manages to swim to shore, and the local people feed and protect the bird until its new feathers grow in where the old ones fell out. There is a parallel for those of us who are transformed by the renewing of our minds. As our old negative ways are stripped from us, pristine feathers of the new nature appear. Thoughts from God emerge from us, and we arise with a refreshing strength and restored vitality.

NOT ALONE ON THE JOURNEY

The lordship of Jesus is how we navigate life. He proclaimed, "I am the way, and the truth, and the life; no one comes to the Father, but by me."[14] Other versions translate "way" as a path or road. As we learned earlier from Proverbs 3:5 and 6, when we acknowledge God in all our ways, he will make our paths smooth. God sent his son to get rid of the obstacles hindering our access to the Father. Under Jesus' lordship, our journey through life is smooth. It is through him that we grow into the most meaningful relationship with God.

Paul later wrote, "In the same way you received Jesus our Lord and Messiah by faith, continue your journey of faith, progressing further into your union with him!"[15] The connotation of "received" in this verse includes *being joined to or becoming a companion with another*. Recall that Romans 10 discusses how this is done. "And if you confess with your mouth our Lord Jesus and you believe in your heart that God raised him from the dead, you will have life. For the heart that believes in him is justified and the mouth that confesses him has life."[16] These verses provide two simple actions people can take to receive anything from God. First, we confess; and second, we believe in our hearts. To "confess" means to agree with, or say the same thing as another. When it comes to the things of God, we are to line up both our thoughts and words with his "higher" ways. (Isaiah reveals God's heart. "'My thoughts are nothing like your thoughts,' says the Lord. 'And my ways are far beyond anything you could imagine. For just as the heavens are higher than the earth, so my ways are higher than your ways and my thoughts higher than your thoughts.'"[17]) Secondly, to "believe in the heart" indicates trust in the integrity of God's thoughts and words with all of our innermost being. We become born again believers and then we continue to confess who we are in him while really believing it with all of our hearts. This begins and prospers our journey with him.

Jesus graciously sends this invitation to "whoevers" everywhere. "Come to me, all you who are weary and burdened, and I will give you rest. Take my yoke on you and learn from me, because I am gentle and humble in heart, and you will find rest for your souls. For my yoke is easy to bear, and my load is not hard to carry."[18] Over the years, I have heard different explanations of what this yoke means. Some believe it is associated with a rabbi's teachings of God and the yoke identifies them with their disciples. Others suggest that it was worn at ancient ceremonies and signified the student-teacher relationship and the discipline of their studies. This symbol of the yoke may still be seen at academic graduations where it is worn over the gown of both the students and their teachers. But I understood the yoke best when I became friends with a group of farmers.

After graduating culinary school many years ago, I felt equipped to work in any restaurant. But before settling into a job, I decided to take a road trip and traveled halfway across the United States. On the way back home, as my travel funds evaporated, I took a two-week job as a server at the local eatery of a small town in Ohio. The first day of work seemed like I was walking onto a movie set of a typical American small town off-the-highway restaurant. I was behind the counter, hustling back and forth to serve customers who were perched on their swivel stools, eyeballing my every move. Most of them were farmers who had come in from their early morning chores to eat breakfast, catch up on neighborhood news and exchange agricultural advice.

One of the customers, with a slight stutter said, "Give me some c-c-coffee w-w-with cream." Now I don't know whether it was his speech impediment or my overconfidence in discerning a Midwestern accent. Possibly I had developed a selective hearing problem during my training in French wait-service at culinary school. Perhaps it was a combination of all of the above. But I could have sworn he said, "Coffee with whipped cream."

I gently brought his cup of hot brew in for a smooth landing right before his anticipating eyes, eager to please the customer. Then, as if by magic, I produced a can of whipped cream out from behind my back. Displaying professional finesse, I removed the cap and swirled a beautiful mound of white delicacy on top of his coffee. Silence fell upon the chattering crowd. All eyes were riveted on me, and my confident grin quickly gave way to chagrin as the stuttering farmer exclaimed, "W-w-what in the hell are you d-d-doing?" Another farmer firmly interrogated, "Boy? Are you new in this town?" I silently told God, "I'm so intimidated—and this is only the first day. What do I say? What do I do?" Inspired perhaps by that sense of being on the set of a movie, I produced my best John Wayne imitation: "Nope. Just passing through." They all roared with laughter, and from that moment on I became one of the boys.

During my brief stay in the town, my new farmer friends shared with me that before tractors became popular, they used horses to plow the fields. The seasoned, more experienced animals knew the lay of the land from plowing it over many planting seasons. The horses intuitively pulled harder going uphill and through rocky soil, yet were gentle to not disrupt tender plants as they plowed out the weeds. A younger, less experienced animal got easily sidetracked, wanted to go in its own direction or even stopped to eat the crops. The farmers continued explaining that a yoke was placed on both the experienced and the young horse to connect them together. This way the mature animal trained its immature counterpart how to navigate and work the land. Sometimes the younger horse might try to stop, or stray in another direction. Nevertheless, the seasoned animal firmly kept the pace, pulled the other horse along, and stayed on the right path.

Jesus beckons us to be yoked with him and learn from him. Paul understood this when he wrote, "Follow my example, as I follow the example of Christ." He also declared, "Join together in following my example, brothers and sisters, and just as you have us as a model, keep your eyes on those who live as we do."[19] In today's vernacular a disciple is called an "apprentice." Jesus is called the Master. When we confess him as Lord, we enter into a relationship with him where he personally teaches us how to skillfully journey through life, the best life. You are not alone on this journey

This journey is not without obstacles. The epistle of Ephesians exhorts, "Finally, grow powerful in union with the Lord, in union with his mighty strength! Use all the armor and weaponry that God provides, so that you will be able to stand against the deceptive tactics of the Adversary. For we are not struggling against human beings, but against the rulers, authorities and cosmic powers governing this darkness, against the spiritual forces of evil in the heavenly realm."[20] The Scriptures declare we have an enemy, the devil. But believers can stand against his attacks by putting on the whole armor of God. This includes putting on the mind of Christ and walking by the Spirit—walking in love. No wonder Paul exclaimed, "Yet even in the midst of all these things, we triumph over them all, for God has made us to be more than conquerors, and his demonstrated love is our glorious victory over everything!"[21]

One of the most destructive devices in the devil's arsenal is temptation. This is a topic about which there is much misunderstanding. The next chapter reveals how a true understanding about temptation actually reduces stress and keeps us on the road to victorious living.

References

1. Romans 13:8, 10 (NIV); Galatians 5:14 (NIV); James 2:8 (NIV); 1 Corinthians 13:8a (EXB) and Galatians 5:16 (NIV)

2. Galatians 5:22-23 (GW); Galatians 2:20 (TLB) and taken from Luke 9:23

3. Referenced from Romans 8:5-8

4. Romans 8:12 (NLT)

5. Romans 13:14 (NIV)

6. Romans 12:1-2 (NET)

7. Romans 8:14 and 2 Corinthians 3:17 (WEB)

8. 2 Corinthians 10:4-5 (APNT)

9. Philippians 2:13 (NLT)

10. Romans 8:28-29 (NET)

11. James 1:17b

12. 1 Corinthians 2:16 (NLT) and Philippians 2:5 (NLT)

13. Isaiah 40:31(NET)

14. John 14:6 (RSV)

15. Colossians 2:6 (TPT)

16. Romans 10:9, 10 (APNT)

17. Isaiah 55:8-9 (NLT)

18. Matthew 11:28-30 (NET)

19. 1 Corinthians 11:1 and Philippians 3:17 (NIV)

20. Ephesians 6:10-12 (CJB)

21. Romans 8:37 (TPT)

CHAPTER 13

OVERCOMING TEMPTATION

There is a widespread belief that God places various circumstances in the lives of believers to quantify their loyalty to him or build their character. The terms "testing" and "trials" are often used synonymously with "temptation" to describe this so-called divine intervention. Yet the Book of James is clear when it states, "And remember, when you are being tempted, do not say, 'God is tempting me.' God is never tempted to do wrong, and he never tempts anyone else." Therefore, if God does not tempt us, where does temptation come from?

The gospel records of Matthew 4 and Luke 4 both affirm that the devil causes temptation. He is even called "the tempter." In the garden of Eden, God made a perfect environment for his creation. There was no sin, sickness or stress. Then the devil introduced temptation, and it led to the fall of humankind. That is when sin, sickness and stress entered the world and sadly remain prevalent today.

God is good; he invites each "whoever" to explore his goodness. The Psalmist implores us, "Open your mouth and taste, open your eyes and see—how good God is. Blessed are you who run to him" Notice it says, run *to* him and not away from him. This is God's invitation to experience his approachability and trustworthiness. Another Psalm amplifies this thought: "For the Lord is always good and ready to receive you. He's so loving that it will amaze you—so kind that it will astound you! And he is famous for his faithfulness toward all. Everyone knows our God can be trusted, for he keeps his promises to every generation!" Trust comes from knowing God experientially, and knowing him experientially comes by spending time with him in the *God Place*. He never devises ways to tempt anyone, but rather he delights in ways to bless those who trust in him. "'For I know what I have planned for you,' says the Lord. 'I have plans to prosper you, not to harm you. I have plans to give you a future filled with hope.'" Additionally, John's third epistle emphasizes that God's heartfelt desire is for his children to prosper and be healthy.[1]

Regardless of these promises, there are those who still believe God puts them through special seasons of discipline to mold their character. Yet Paul asserts, "But remember this—the wrong desires that come into your life aren't anything new and different. Many others have faced exactly the same problems before you. And no temptation is irresistible. You can trust God to keep the temptation from becoming so strong that you can't stand up against it, for he has promised this and will do what he says. He will show you how to escape temptation's power so that you can bear up patiently against it." God does not tempt with sin, sickness or stress in order to humble us, teach us a lesson or require some proof of our faithfulness to him. If that was his nature, then Jesus acted contrary to his Father's intentions. "You know that God anointed Jesus from Nazareth with the Holy Spirit and with power. Jesus went everywhere and did good things, such as healing everyone who was under the devil's power. Jesus did these things because God was with him." The devil is behind temptation, sin, sickness and stress; not God.[2]

Just because someone is tempted doesn't mean they have sinned.

EVERYONE EXPERIENCES TEMPTATION

Everyone experiences temptation. But it is *how* we respond to temptation that determines the outcome. A common confusion exists in understanding the difference between temptation and sin. They are not the same. The Book of Hebrews says of Jesus, "For we have not a high priest who is unable to sympathize with our weaknesses, but one who in every respect has been tempted as we are, yet without sin." Jesus was indeed tempted, yet he never yielded to any temptation to the degree of sinning. Therefore, just because someone is tempted doesn't mean they have sinned.

The Book of James expounds on this idea: "But each person is tempted when he is lured and enticed by his own desire. Then desire when it has conceived gives birth to sin; and sin when it is full-grown brings forth death." Think about how a fish is innocently attracted to the alluring bait and then hooked. The word "desire" could be translated *lust* or *passion*. When believers relentlessly pursue suggestions of self-centered desires, they are lured away from their identity and purpose as sons or daughters of God. Their worldly cravings bring forth sin resulting in separation from God in their minds.

James addresses the topic of temptation right at the beginning of his letter. "Count it all joy, my brothers, when you fall into various temptations." The New Living Translation renders the same passage, "Dear brothers and sisters, when troubles of any kind come your way, consider it an opportunity for great joy." Recall that the Old Testament Scriptures use the words "trouble" and "distress" interchangeably; therefore, temptations are stressful. To "fall into" is defined as *to come across* or *be encompassed by* something. In other words, it happens because we live in a fallen world. But if temptations are stressful, and the source of them are from the devil, why does James instruct believers to consider it "all joy?" The next verse reveals the answer. "You know these prove your faith. It helps you not to give up." To *know* is to become familiar with through experience. To *prove* is to sample, with the intent of approval. For example, when new products are rolled out into the market, manufacturers heavily advertise the features and benefits of those products. Frequently, coupons are distributed to encourage consumers to try the products. The strategy of the manufacturer is not for the customer to disapprove the products, but that they experience and prove the manufacturers meant what they promised. These practices increase consumer confidence and approval.[3]

PUT TO THE TEST

The experience of the proving of our faith produces patient endurance. This tenacity does not emerge from our own capacity to grit our teeth and bear it but from God. Colossians explains that believers are "strengthened with all power, according to his glorious might, for all endurance and patience with joy, giving thanks to the Father." Peter expands this thought. "In this you greatly rejoice, even though now for a little while, if necessary, you have been distressed by various trials, so that the proof of your faith, being more precious than gold which is perishable, even though tested by fire, may be found to result in praise and glory and honor at the revelation of Jesus Christ."[4] God is our source of strength, endurance, patience and joy during our stressful times. As God liberates us from stress, we respond by giving thanks. Expecting and then realizing God's deliverance purifies our hearts while increasing our trust in him.

Proverbs offers this analogy. "The refining pot is for silver and the furnace for gold, but the Lord tests hearts." This verse compares testing the human heart with the refining of precious metals whereby impurities are burned off. A similar metaphor is recorded in the gospels where John the Baptist spoke of an eminent baptism greater than water. It is termed the baptism of Holy Spirit and fire where chaff, the unusable part of the wheat, is burned up. This testing is a refinement or purifying of our faith which emanates from the heart. As faith is refined, our hearts are purified from the old nature and our minds are renewed improving the course of our lives. As this transformation occurs, we prove and approve God will. When we encounter problems, we are confident God will provide us with the resources to endure the situation. Our rescue from temptation and its accompanying stress is solely dependent upon him.[5]

Patience refines and proves the faith in our hearts. It is the indicator of our trust in God. It is a fruit of the Spirit. Proving God in every area of our lives develops an enduring expectation that he will get us through any temptation thrown our way. No wonder we are encouraged to express joy when we fall into temptation. We simply go to God and exclaim, "You are faithful and your promises are true!" We adopt this victorious lifestyle by putting our faith to the test and then beholding the delivering hand of God.

REFUSING TO DOUBT

James offers more insight and a caution regarding this patient endurance.

"So let it grow, and don't try to squirm out of your problems. For when your patience is finally in full bloom, then you will be ready for anything, strong in character, full and complete. If you want to know what God wants you to do, ask him, and he will gladly tell you, for he is always ready to give a bountiful supply of wisdom to all who ask him; he will not resent it. But when you ask him, be sure that you really expect him to tell you, for a doubtful mind will be as unsettled as a wave of the sea that is driven and tossed by the wind; and every decision you then make will be uncertain, as you turn first this way and then that. If you don't ask with faith, don't expect the Lord to give you any solid answer."[6]

In this passage, believers are instructed to go to the *God Place* and ask for wisdom and help when dealing with temptation. But James reminds his readers to offer their petitions to God with confidence and trust, and not waver between believing his promises and the evidence of circumstances. Such fluctuation produces doubt, and this uncertainty is contrasted to faith. Doubt decays the promises of God, but faith, accompanied by enduring patience, faith, which ripens those promises into a bounty of fruitful outcomes.

Jesus taught his disciples, his apprentices, "Have faith in God. Truly, I say to you, whoever says to this mountain, 'Be taken up and thrown into the sea,' and does not doubt in his heart, but believes that what he says will come to pass, it will be done for him. Therefore I tell you, whatever you ask in prayer, believe that you have received it, and it will be yours."[7] The mountain referred to in Jesus' teaching represents any stressful problem a person encounters. Jesus invites the "whoever" to prove this promise. Jesus' instructions are to trust in God, speak to the problem, tell it to go and refuse to doubt in our hearts. Then with faith, we are to confess God's promises of deliverance from the problem with full expectation that we will reap the proclaimed result. When we go to God and put our trust in him, we will absolutely receive our answer and the wisdom to overcome any temptation. As we patiently endure temptation from the enemy, we abound in faith. Like the eagle that mounts up with renewed and strengthened wings, we gloriously emerge from each challenge as victorious conquerors.

RECOGNIZING AND REFUTING THE DEVIL'S SCHEMES

Much like a boxer who keeps pounding away at an opponent's injury, the devil tempts us where we are the weakest. Right after Jesus was baptized, God, with an audible voice from heaven, announced to everyone Jesus was his beloved son and that he was delighted and pleased with him.[8] Jesus had not performed any miracles or works of wonder as of yet. The truth alone that Jesus was God's son brought delightful pleasure to his heavenly Father. Then the Spirit of God led Jesus into the wilderness where he was tempted by the devil. Jesus fasted for 40 days and became extremely hungry. The devil (also called the tempter) approached Jesus and said, "If you are the Son of God, command these stones to become bread." Jesus responded, "The Scripture says, 'A person cannot live on bread alone but on every word that comes from God's mouth.'" Even though the Father had just called Jesus his "beloved Son," the devil tempted

Jesus by questioning his identity. The devil's motive is to constantly undermine the foundational truths that God *is* love, and God *is* good. He *always cares* for *everyone*. That includes the "whoever." The devil's suggestion that Jesus command the stones to be transformed into bread subtly insinuated that God must have brought Jesus out into the wilderness only to abandon him in his great time of need! "Jesus, you're so hungry," Satan implied. "How are you going to save the world if you fall over dead from starvation? Apparently, your Father isn't taking very good care of you, so you better take care of yourself." The intent of this temptation was to attack and belittle God's integrity and provision for his beloved while attempting to pressure Jesus into a self-centered survival mode.

> *Satan magnified a need while slandering God's responsiveness to that need. Then, he suggested the solution lied in independence from God.*

The tempter's methods are nothing new. This was the identical tactic used by the devil to beguile Eve. Satan magnified a need while slandering God's responsiveness to that need. Then, he suggested the solution lied in independence from God—which is anything but the solution. The devil relentlessly persists in tempting us in like manner today. Satan was arrogant enough to tempt Jesus. Let's be aware of his endeavors to do the same to us also.

Jesus countered the tempter with the reasoning of God. People require food and other physical sustenance to live, but their deepest need is to live by every word that proceeds (present tense) from God.[9] Jesus uttered only what his Father gave him to speak. He therefore must have asked God how to respond to the temptation, waiting for heavenly guidance in what to speak and do. He didn't deal with the devil by relying on his vast intellect or knowledge of the Scriptures but totally depended on the guidance of his Father. How many of us run after the words, advice and counsel of others yet neglect to seek God first? Jesus' example exemplifies the vital importance for us to receive and declare every word that steadily flows from God in our times of temptation. The greatest temptation of humankind is to attempt resolving problems without God.

Satan's temptations fall under two categories: pressure or pleasure. Jesus illuminated this truth in his story about the sower. When the sower spread the seed, some of it fell on rocky soil. When the seed sprouted, it dried up because it lacked moisture from the soil. Jesus compares this seed to people who joyfully receive the word from God, but they believe for only a little while because they have no root. In their time of temptation, their trust in God's promises fails. Jesus also points out their endurance is short-lived and unstable. Pressures cause them to stumble as offenses of distress, ill-treatment and hostility uproot their shallow faith. This parable offers more lessons for those who have ears to hear. Jesus explains that some of the sower's seed was dispersed among thorns. The thorns grew among the young plants and choked them. Jesus compares this seed to those who also heard the words from God but are choked with worldly cares, the deceitfulness of riches and the pleasures of this life. It is clear that God's word was heard and initially received, yet fruitful results were hindered. Why? Those hearing and receiving became distracted by the world's pressures and pleasures, diverting their focus.[10] As we become aware of Satan's schemes of pressure and pleasure, we will recognize the bait and not be distracted. Instead, we will ask God for wisdom and receive his strategy to successfully stand against the attacks of the devil.

PERSONAL, POWERFUL ACCESS TO GOD

In addition to this awareness, a realization of our *access* to God gives us strength and hope when facing temptation. When Jesus was tempted in the garden of Gethsemane, he cried, "Abba, Father, all things are possible for you." Abba is an endearing, intimate and respectful title for God as a heavenly Father. Our rights as children of God and our access to him include this relational affinity where we, too, may call him Abba. In fact, we have the same Spirit as Jesus Christ, and that Spirit cries out to God, "Abba Father." Because we are God's sons or daughters through Christ, we have the same personal access to the Father as Jesus does. We have this access because we are one with Christ. Through this access we discover we are cherished with the same degree of love that Abba Father has for his Son. Jesus confirmed this when he prayed to his Abba Father. "I am in them and you are in me. May they experience such perfect unity that the world will know that you sent me and that you love them as much as you love me."[11]

Not only is our access to God personal, it is powerful. Romans tells us, "Being therefore justified by faith, we have peace with God through our Lord Jesus Christ; through whom we also have our access by faith into this grace in which we stand. We rejoice in hope of the glory of God."[12] Accepting and trusting in the name of Jesus Christ and his accomplishments on our behalf grants us access into the *God Place*. This is where the Father's grace and presence are discovered as we stand in awe of his love for us. Released from the burden and debt of guilt and shame, we walk in our newfound freedom and respond to God with loving praise in return. His love energizes our faith so that our hearts are purified, our minds are renewed and our lives are transformed.

His love energizes our faith so that our hearts are purified, our minds are renewed and our lives are transformed.

It is our privilege to enjoy this access. I remember when a friend gifted me a private VIP "access pass" to a lounge at an international airport. Having a five-hour layover after a nine-hour flight, I was ready to receive all the benefits the lounge had to offer! Once inside, I realized my access included free (and unlimited) food and beverages, comfortable chairs and hot showers with complimentary toiletries. This relaxing haven was a sanctuary of peace and quiet, sheltered from the noisy hustle and bustle occurring in the common areas of the airport. But it was up to me to use the access pass. I could have chosen to not go in. Likewise, it is up to us whether or not we use the access we've been gifted. Sometimes we do not think we are worthy to access God's presence. This delusion is caused when we focus on our shortcomings rather than recognizing the merits of Jesus Christ's accomplishments. Accessing God's loving presence provides us with rest, peace and hope as he guarantees his promise of deliverance from our temptation. Here we find the most benevolent blessings of the *God Place!*

It is also vital to understand that our access to God is not restricted, limited or categorized. All who believe in Jesus have access regardless of race, gender, class, economic background, education, level of intelligence, political party or even professed religious affiliation. Access to God is available to the "whoevers" who believe on the Lord Jesus Christ. God does not prefer one person over another. Ephesians states that all of us who believe have access "by one Spirit" to the Father. This refers to the Spirit nature that was lost through Adam but restored to us through Christ Jesus. It is one Spirit for all of humankind. This is another accomplishment of Christ for "whoevers." Ephesians also announces, "For he himself is our peace, who has made the two groups one and has destroyed the barrier, the dividing wall of hostility." While the "two groups" in this verse refers to Jews and Gentiles, it extends to all the "whoevers" in Christ. In him, there are no systematized layers of comparison, judgmentalism, competition or rank. This is another wonderful blessing of the new nature. As Galatians declares, "And we no longer see each other in our former state—Jew or non-Jew, rich or poor, male or female—because we're all one through our union with Jesus Christ

> *Access to God is available to the "whoevers" who believe on the Lord Jesus Christ. God does not prefer one person over another.*

with no distinction between us."[13]

This undeniably asserts that all prejudice, racism, chauvinism, sexism, political bias, extreme nationalism or any other discriminatory wall is destroyed through Christ. Furthermore, as we realize that God loves all "whoevers" equally, we begin to tear down those barriers that have been subtly but unmistakably constructed in our hearts. We grow in the acceptance of being unified by the Holy Spirit with our common bond being the lordship of Jesus Christ. Remember, our access is not the result of our good works, or affiliation with an organization or a church, or with an official document or a person's endorsement. It is *only* because of Christ Jesus. Understanding our access to God helps us when we are under temptation by imploring us to come to God without the hesitation or hindrance. So often, when we focus on ourselves or dwell on our assumptions of how others perceive us, we forget this wonderful access. Our privileged access is the purity of the *God Place*!

BOLDNESS TO SEEK HIS HELP

Ephesians informs us that our access to God is accompanied by boldness and confidence.[14] Boldness is the absence of fear in speaking; it brings free communication and cheerful conversation. This boldness is now ours, bought by the blood of Jesus Christ, and our access brings us into the *God Place* where there is no fear or intimidation. Why? Because when God sees each of us, he sees his son or daughter in the completeness and oneness of his beloved firstborn, Jesus Christ. Jesus is the chosen one whom God has made Lord over all things both in heaven and in earth.

God's love for us is so incredibly penetrating that fear is totally obliterated in his presence. This is why the last place the devil wants you to go when you are tempted is the *God Place*. In this secure place we don't trust in our own good works, reputation, abilities, talents, accomplishments or even the acceptance of others. We lean *only* on the accomplishments of Jesus Christ. He paid the price for our access. Now it is up to us to boldly and confidently use it.

What do we do once we access the presence of God? We freely pour out our hearts before him, listen to his counsel and deeply commune, enjoying rich fellowship with our Father. God's inviting heart cries out to us, "My beloved children, your hearts will no longer condemn you when you realize that you are clean before me. You were bought back from the slavery of sin by the blood of my Son. So now, come to me and speak freely with confidence. This is my gift of grace to you. I welcome you. Please come, sit down, and let's have a friendly chat."

The first Epistle of John discusses the joy of fellowship. "Truly our fellowship is with the Father, and with his Son Jesus Christ." Fellowship is not just with God or with Jesus: it is with both of them! Part of this fellowship with them is their willingness and ability to help us. We already discovered that we are identified with Christ, but the Book of Hebrews informs us that Jesus Christ is identified with us, too. "We have a chief priest who is able to sympathize with our weaknesses. He was tempted in every way that we are, but he didn't sin" and, "For because he himself has suffered when tempted, he is able to help those who are being tempted." Our Lord Jesus Christ identifies with everything we go through, absolutely everything! He felt every kind of human suffering when he was led into the wilderness and tempted of the devil. He always emerged victorious, even when he went to the cross to pay the price for our redemption. Unlike any other person, he knows exactly what it takes for you to patiently endure your situation.

No wonder Hebrews encourages us, "Let us then with confidence draw near to the throne of grace, that we may receive mercy and find grace to help in time of need." We can find help in the time of need—before we stumble. For example, consider the ancient nautical practice of "frapping." Frapping involved the use of rope or cable bindings to strengthen or reinforce parts of a ship that are under great strain. In the Book of Acts, Luke refers to frapping in his narration of a ship's crew using helps to undergird the ship and prevent it from falling apart.[15] When life seems to be falling apart from the storms of circumstances or temptation, Jesus helps to undergird us, hold us together and sustain us as we surmount our difficulties. His guidance navigates us into a safe haven where we come confidently unto God's throne room of grace. When we boldly approach God during temptation, he will bring us through the storm while using the trial to strengthen our faith and glorify him.

An acquaintance of mine used to pastor a church in California where he felt things were growing wonderfully. He and his family were blessed. This gentleman accepted an invitation to preach at a church in a neighboring state, and at the end of the visit was asked by the hosting pastor, who was planning to move on to other ministry work, if he'd consider relocating there to become the church's next pastor. After thinking about it for a year, he finally accepted the new position—convinced in his heart that God had confirmed the move.

But there was a problem. The church's members voted him in by a slim margin, meaning he was walking into a divided congregation. Before long, the number of people attending the church dwindled in half, down to just a few hundred. People left nasty notes on the windshield of his car, and sometimes even stood up and said, "I didn't vote for you. I hate you!" as he walked down the aisle after service. The temptation to quit haunted him as he felt the relentless pressure of rejection. Meanwhile, he had received offers to go elsewhere and enjoy a better salary, a bigger church and a markedly friendlier congregation. But as my friend sought the Lord's counsel, God told him to stay because he wanted to do extraordinary things at that church through him.

What happened? Today, that church conducts three services each Sunday with over two thousand people attending each service.

It has multiple programs to help meet the congregation's needs and reaches out to its surrounding community. He told me what he learned through the experience: "If we are not watchful, we will let circumstances and the influences of others rob us of our God-given destiny. Don't let your emotions steal the blessings of your calling. Stay where he's called you to be. Don't give up on the dream that God has embedded in your heart, but submit it back to him. He cares more about your heart than the dream he's put in it." He concluded, "He's right there in the midst of our challenges. He goes through the dark nights with us, holding our hand. Remain faithful and he will lead you. Every glory has a story!"

CONFESS TO BE FORGIVEN

There may be times when we succumb to the pressures or pleasures of temptation. God informs us what to do in those circumstances.

John, one of the original twelve apostles who sat at Jesus' feet, was present for the first outpouring of the Holy Spirit, and lived well into the early days of the first-century church. He offered insight into this topic when he wrote his first epistle. It was written to the believers of that time so that they could have fellowship with him—and with other believers, whose fellowship was also with the Father and his Son Jesus Christ. Fellowship involves both relational sharing and mutual participation. It begins with vertical fellowship by individually going to our *God Place*, and overflows into a horizontal fellowship with others in a community *God Place* where we freely gather with those who also fellowship with the Father and his Son. John anticipated that the outcome of this fellowship was that their "joy may be full." Fellowship and joy with each other in the presence of God is his ideal state for us. When we yield to temptation our fellowship is broken and our joy thwarted. We find ourselves walking in darkness. In his letter John continued, "God is light, and in Him is no darkness at all. If we say that we have fellowship with Him and [*at the same time*] we walk in the darkness, *then* we lie and we do not practice the truth [*in our walk*]. On the other hand, if we walk in the light as He is, *then* in the light we have fellowship with one another, and the blood of Jesus, His Son, cleanses us from every sin."

There is a solution to yielding to temptation "If we confess our sins, he is faithful and just to forgive us our sins and to cleanse us from all unrighteousness." To *confess* something is to say the same thing God says about it. What does God say about our sins? They will be forgiven because he is faithful and just to forgive them. Remember that when Jesus went to the cross, we were saved from sin and forgiven of sins. John's epistle is written to born again believers and therefore addresses sin as it pertains to a son or daughter of God breaking fellowship. As we confess that God is faithful to forgive us, we are cleansed. *Cleansing* is a refreshing concept. It is in the present tense and reflects the imagery of a gentle heavenly rain or a cascading waterfall. This epistle continues to encourage the believer: "Because if our heart condemns us, how much greater [is] God than our heart? And he knows everything. My beloved, if our heart does not condemn us, our faces are open before God, and everything that we ask, we will receive from him, because we keep his commandments and do pleasing [things] before him. And this is his commandment, that we believe on the name of his Son, Jesus Christ, and love one another as he commanded us."

John exhorts us to walk in the light of God and practice righteousness. But if, because of temptation, we sin and our fellowship is broken, we are to confess what God says about sin and we will be forgiven, cleansed and restored back into fellowship. Then, as we grow in acceptance of who we are in Christ and allow him to have preeminence in our lives, we will naturally refrain from those habits and behaviors that cause us to sin. As the apostle John said, "No one who lives deeply in Christ makes a practice of sin. None of those who do practice sin have taken a good look at Christ. They've got him all backward." John elaborated, "No one born of God makes a practice of sinning, for God's seed abides in him, and he cannot keep on sinning, because he has been born of God."[16]

OVERCOMING BY ABIDING

In the Gospel of John, Jesus gave us an epic discourse about abiding.

"I am the true vine, and my Father is the vinedresser. Every branch in me that does not bear fruit he takes away, and every branch that does bear fruit he prunes, that it may bear more fruit. Already you are clean because of the word that I have spoken to you. Abide in me, and I in you. As the branch cannot bear fruit by itself, unless it abides in the vine, neither can you, unless you abide in me. I am the vine; you are the branches. Whoever abides in me and I in him, he it is that bears much fruit, for apart from me you can do nothing. If anyone does not abide in me he is thrown away like a branch and withers; and the branches are gathered, thrown into the fire, and burned. If you abide in me, and my words abide in you, ask whatever you wish, and it will be done for you. By this my Father is glorified, that you bear much fruit and so prove to be my disciples. As the Father has loved me, so have I loved you. Abide in my love. If you keep my commandments, you will abide in my love, just as I have kept my Father's commandments and abide in his love. These things I have spoken to you, that my joy may be in you, and that your joy may be full." [17]

This passage defines our relationship with both the Father and the Son. Jesus is the true vine, his Father is the vinedresser and we are the branches. The true vine is rooted and grounded in love and is the source of nourishment and strength for the branches. Jesus as the true vine is the contact point, and the life of the Holy Spirit flows through the vine and into the branch.

In the second sentence of this discourse the term "takes away" is more accurately rendered "takes up." It alludes to a traditional agricultural practice where farmers considered every branch valuable. The farmer made sure to dredge—to lift up and clean off any branches and leaves that were partially obstructed from the sunlight by the muddy soil. The vine keeper then repositioned the branch and increased its potential to bear fruit. The word "clean" is the same word as "prune" used elsewhere in this passage. It refers to cleansing and trimming away the remnants of the dead old nature so that the branch may flourish and bountifully produce the fruit of the new nature.

As believers, we do not have the resources to bear fruit outside of abiding in Christ. Jesus said he could not do anything of his own initiative, but only what he heard and saw the Father doing. Remember, Jesus modeled how to live by every word presently proceeding from the mouth of God. Jesus taught repeatedly, "The words I say are not my own but are from my Father who lives in me. And he does his work through me. Just believe it—that I am in the Father and the Father is in me. Or else believe it because of the mighty miracles you have seen me do. In solemn truth I tell you, anyone believing in me shall do the same miracles I have done, and even greater ones, because I am going to be with the Father. You can ask him for anything, using my name, and I will do it, for this will bring praise to the Father because of what I, the Son, will do for you. Yes, ask anything, using my name, and I will do it!"

We discovered earlier that our lives are hid in Christ and anything outside of abiding in him is not productive and does not produce fruit. He is our life. Jesus additionally shared this revelation as recorded in John's gospel. "When a man loves me, he follows my teaching. Then my Father will love him, and we will come to that man and make our home within him. The man who does not really love me will not follow my teaching. Indeed, what you are hearing from me now is not really my saying, but comes from the Father who sent me."[18] These verses offer magnificent takeaways. As we abide in the words of the Father and the Son, we will, by our actions carry out the wonderful works of God. This confirms that his words have made their dwelling place in us. Additionally, our confidence will blossom; and we will begin to ask God whatever we desire according to his will. We have been given the authority to use the name of Jesus Christ, and because we are one with him, it shall be done for us. Why? This is how we bear fruit and glorify him. Finally, as we abide in Christ's love, we will naturally love one another with that same love. This further sheds light on the *God Place*, both vertically and horizontally.

As you wander away from the fire, you soon begin to feel the chill and naturally return to the source of your warmth and comfort.

Imagine how much stress is alleviated by abiding in him, his words and his love! This is how you overcome temptation. This is the answer to being rescued from stress! This is the *God Place*. He who faced and conquered every temptation lives in you. He is constantly inviting you to be with him in (you guessed it) the *God Place*! It's much like sitting by a fire on a cold winter's night. As you wander away from the fire, you soon begin to feel the chill and naturally return to the source of your warmth and comfort.

The *God Place* is where you abide in Christ as you realize and experience God's loving presence and care for you. This reality is the greatest way for you to be rescued from stress.

References

1.   James 1:13 (NLT); Psalm 34:8 (MSG); Psalm 100:5 (TPT); Jeremiah 29:11 (NET) and Reference from 3 John 2

2.   1 Corinthians 10:13 (TLB) and Acts 10:38 (GW)

3.   Hebrews 4:15 (RSV); James 1:14-15 (RSV); James 1:2 (WEB, NLT) and James 1:3 (NLV)

4.   Colossians 1:11-12a (ESV) and 1 Peter 1:6-7 (NASB)

5.   Proverbs 17:3 (NAS); Matthew 3:11-12 and Luke 3:16-17

6.   James 1:4-8 (TLB)

7.   Mark 11:22b-24 (ESV)

8. Matthew 3:17b (TLB)
9. Referenced from various translations of Matthew 4:2-4
10. Referenced from various translations of Luke 8:13; Mark 4:17, Luke 8:7, 14; Matthew 13:22 and Mark 4:19
11. Referenced from Mark 14:36a (ESV); Romans 8:15; Galatians 4:6 (RSV) and John 17:23 (NLT)
12. Romans 5:1-2 (WEB)
13. Ephesians 2:18; Ephesians 2:14 (NIV) and Galatians 3:28 (TPT)
14. Ephesians 3:12
15. 1 John 1:3; Hebrews 4:15 (GW); Hebrews 2:18 (ESV); Hebrews 4:16 (ESV); and Acts 27:17 (YLT)
16. Referenced from 1 John 1:3-4; 1 John 1:5b-7 (WT); 1 John 1:9 (ESV); 1 John 3:20-23 (APNT); 1 John 3:6 (MSG) and 1 John 3:9 (ESV)
17. John 15:1-11 (ESV)
18. See John 5:19; 5:30; 7:16; 8:28 and referenced quotations from John 14:10-14 (TLB) and John 14:23-24 (J.B. PHILLIPS)

CHAPTER 14

WHO CARES?

One amazing aspect about writing this book is that it has led me on an unexpected adventure with God. He has given me fresh revelation and understanding to the context of each chapter as the writing has unfolded. Sometimes I personally experienced the relevance of the topic; other times, through what can only be called a divine appointment, I have connected with someone who has.

While writing this particular chapter, I was on a month-long mission trip to Africa and India that included my attendance at a wedding in Kampala, Uganda. The night before my flight, I focused on making sure my luggage was under the 50-pound maximum weight requirement. My suitcases were overstuffed with items given to me by local believers to hand deliver to their families and friends in faraway places. The evening was consumed with other last minute details of the trip, so with little sleep I left for the airport at 4:30 the next morning. Amid the rush, I forgot that my Indian visa was in an older, stamp-filled passport and not in the current passport I had along with me. This error should have been caught when I initially checked in, but the personnel at the airport missed it and allowed me to board the first plane of the series of flights to Africa.

My flight from San Francisco was going to take me to Japan, where I would then catch another flight to India before finally arriving in Africa. When it was discovered in San Francisco that I didn't have my original visa for India, I attempted to show the airline officials a photocopy of it. That did not satisfy their requirements, and they apologetically refused to let me board. My dilemma was compounded because even when I called various agencies to verify the validity of my Indian visa, they all replied that I needed to produce the original document. Now I was forced to somehow acquire the original Indian visa, cancel existing overseas flights and rebook new flights in order to attend the wedding in Africa as planned. *How could all of this be accomplished? Did I need to fly back home to get my Indian visa? Could it be sent to me in California overnight? Where would I spend the night?* All of these questions overwhelmed my brain.

The airline in San Francisco was prepared to impose additional fees as well, but an employee got on the phone with her supervisor and explained that I needed to be in Africa for an important event. Something about me honoring my commitment to make it to the wedding inspired her. She made it her priority to get me on a flight the next day from San Francisco to Tokyo, and then on to India all at no additional charge. This impressive employee sacrificed most of her lunch hour to battle the initial corporate resistance about the extra fees. She even arranged a seat for me on an already overbooked flight from Tokyo to India for the following day. I was amazed, wondering if she might be an angel.

Despite her generosity, the combination of my forgetfulness and the change fees from both the Indian and African airlines (about $600) left me disheartened and disillusioned. My already distracted mind began to unravel as it helplessly protested, *What is going on God? Don't you care about me? Don't you see that I am doing your work?* God interrupted my bellyaching and quickly reminded me that I sounded like Martha from the scriptural story recorded in Luke. The fact that I had brought along a book about that very passage was providential. The book accurately reflected what I was experiencing, and how I was responding to the stressful circumstances that came crashing in, one wave after another.

PRIORITIES AND PEACE

Let's look at the story of Martha (and Mary, too): "As Jesus and his disciples went on their way, he came to a village where a woman named Martha welcomed him in her home. She had a sister named Mary, who sat down at the feet of the Lord and listened to his teaching. Martha was upset over all the work she had to do, so she came and said, 'Lord, don't you care that my sister has left me to do all the work by myself? Tell her to come and help me!' The Lord answered her, 'Martha, Martha! You are worried and troubled over so many things, but just one is needed. Mary has chosen the right thing, and it will not be taken away from her.'"[1] This narrative is about priorities. Mary chose to sit at Jesus's feet. This custom indicated that she not only desired to hear what he taught but also to practice and apply it. Martha, on the other hand, was more concerned about her service. It wasn't that she didn't love Jesus, she was simply distracted with all the details of hospitality. Her focus had subtly shifted away from the Lord—and consequently, her *God Place*. Her activities were of such importance to her that she even interrupted Jesus and demanded he tell her sister to get up and help her. Her service to others was a horizontal, person-to-person reflection of her love of God. However, it never should have occurred at the expense of her vertical, person-to-God expression of her love for him.

One of our biggest challenges is prioritizing our vertical relationship with God above our horizontal relationships with others. Caught up in the immediate and urgent circumstances of her service, Martha actually allowed her mind to think the Lord did not care about her or what she was doing. She felt like she had been left to carry the burdens of service alone. Her focus was on herself. Jesus told Martha that she was "worried and troubled." Martha had a turbulent and confused mind. Perhaps she thought she was doing God's will, yet the warning signs of stress and frustration proved she had wandered from her *God Place*.

When we feel stressed and begin questioning God's loving care for us, we have allowed circumstances to distract us from his peaceful presence and faithful care. Losing our peace activates a warning light. It starts flashing and sounding an alert signal that we cannot afford to ignore. The presence of stress cautions us to stop what we're doing and resort to the *God Place*. The Epistle of Colossians exhorts, "And let the peace of God rule in your hearts."[2] One way to understand the word "rule" in this verse is to think of the act of umpiring or officiating. When we breach his peace, our divine referee shouts, "Time out! Sit on the bench."

One of our biggest challenges is prioritizing our vertical relationship with God above our horizontal relationships with others.

DISTANCING OURSELVES FROM DISTRACTIONS

Challenged by God with the drama of Mary and Martha, I lamented, "Why didn't you remind me to bring the Indian visa so I could bypass all this aggravation and expense?"

His response was unexpectedly prompt. "Why didn't you ask?"

Although it was delivered gently, God's reply pierced my heart. I realized that in my last minute scurrying to pack, I had disconnected from hearing his voice. I never even asked him if I had forgotten anything. He then added, "How will you grow if you are never challenged to depend on me?" I understood God was not the cause of the situation, and the devil could not be assigned the blame either. "It's me, Oh Lord!"

Yet I also saw that God's *care* was greater than my *carelessness*. *As he cares more*, I thought, *I care less because he has invited me to throw all my cares on him*. I knew I had to own up to my responsibility and not place the blame on anyone or anything for my blunder. God also assured me that he saw this event coming long before it unfolded. He had devised a plan to help me overcome the situation. Suddenly I realized, similar to Abraham, God was encouraging me to increase my faith. That is why he had my "angel" show up.

Trying to find a peaceful spot in an airport is like trying to dance a waltz at a discotheque. I discovered a slightly less congested area in the terminal where I could go to my *God Place*. The surroundings still tried to hinder my efforts. The visible pace of urgency, coupled with passengers scrambling to catch their flights, threatened to disrupt my tranquility. All around me, the constant buzz of busyness and the long lines of people jostling for position intensified the travelers' self-centeredness. This atmosphere bred rudeness, pushiness and other discourteous behaviors. Wearied passengers with underfed bodies and soaring levels of cortisol displayed their unraveled nerves as their travel fatigue was amplified by this confusing environment. Even the soft, soothing music piped throughout the airport was constantly interrupted by frequent announcements. It was challenging to listen to the announcements as people, oblivious to their surroundings, chattered loudly on their cellphones.

Staying positive and being thankful in this stress-filled arena of confusion would determine the difference and decide the outcome.

As I continued to observe the anxiety surrounding me, it became evident that these negative assaults were trying to steal my peace and distract me from what God was saying to me. The moment escalated into a spiritual battle of the mind. I needed to deliberately and aggressively combat these thoughts by seeking his comfort, wisdom, counsel and peace at my *God Place*. Rather than focusing on the seemingly endless negatives, I had to pursue and recognize God's goodness. Staying positive and being thankful in this stress-filled arena of confusion would determine the difference and decide the outcome.

173

As I centered my mind on God, I began to think about the disciples of Christ. Time after time, he demonstrated miracles right before their eyes as they witnessed his life firsthand. For example, according to Mark 4 (and the parallel records in Matthew and Luke), Jesus told the disciples to enter their boat and cross over to the other side of the Sea of Galilee. This was a promise of destiny. Many of the disciples were professional fishermen who knew that severe storms could suddenly arise upon the Galilee out of nowhere. As Jesus napped in the back of the boat, one such tempest rolled in and turbulent waves pounded against the ship, swamping it with water. The storm was so violent the disciples became afraid and woke up their master. "Don't you *care* that we are going to die?" they pleaded. Undisturbed by the squall, Jesus was more concerned with the disciples' response to their surroundings. He rebuked the wind and commanded the sea to calm. As the environment became serene, he asked his disciples why they were so intimidated. Where was their faith?

Their faith had been overwhelmed by fear. Fear is often our response as we evaluate situations through our five senses alone. It results in a maze of confusion, doubt, worry and unbelief. On the other hand, faith means to have trust, confidence and belief in what we have been promised by God and not in what we perceive. God is love, and love energizes faith, which vanquishes tormenting fear. Let's be aware and willing to run to the *God Place* the moment fear attempts to challenge our faith.

Jesus trusted his heavenly Father in every circumstance. That is why he could sleep in the middle of the storm. He knew the words from the Psalms and Proverbs and their promises of restful sleep. "When you lie down, you will not be afraid; When you lie down, your sleep will be sweet;" "I lay down and slept, yet I woke up in safety, for the Lord was watching over me;" "I will lie down and sleep peacefully, for you, Lord, make me safe and secure."[3]

The remembrance of that calm after the storm began hushing my mind as I turned my heart to God. Still, my concentration wavered because of the airport environment, saturated with folks who felt they were the center of the universe, disregarding the need to be courteous to their fellow travelers. When I asked God what fostered this kind of contemptuous conduct, he replied that many are driven by the misconception that "time is money" and reminded me that the power to produce wealth comes from him. Our trust in him is not gauged by our financial status or whether or not things seem to be going well. Rather, trust is exemplified during the whirlwind of life when our faith is strengthened. We hold on to his promises instead of attempting to futilely figure out our problems apart from him.

WALKING AWAY FROM WORRY

While maintaining my *God Place* in the busy airport, I began thinking about another important lesson taught by Jesus. He began by teaching, "no one can serve two masters," referring to God versus material things. He followed that point with the admonition that they were not to be anxious about the cares of life, including eating, drinking or clothing their bodies. Jesus emphasized that life consisted of more than these things. He told them to be aware of greed in their hearts and to be thankful for what they have. Life was not to be measured by the amount of material things they possessed. Next, Jesus told the crowd to observe the birds in the sky and of how God took care of them. They were never stressed about what they were going to eat, but instead offered melodic praise to their Creator every day. Jesus assured his audience that they were much more important to God than birds.

> *Our trust in him is not gauged by our financial status or whether or not things seem to be going well.*

After asking his listeners the rhetorical question, "Which one of you can extend even a moment of your life span through worrying?"

he explained how his heavenly Father clothed the grass of the field with beautiful flowers more glorious than any royal apparel. He asked, "Will not God also clothe his children?" Jesus challenged the people to have more faith in God. He reminded his audience again, "Don't be anxious about the necessities of life." Jesus taught us that worry was what constantly consumed the thoughts of those who did not know of or believe in the one true God. Jesus continued, the concept of a loving and trustworthy God was foreign to the unbelievers. They just could not wrap their heads around the possibility of enjoying a relationship with a God who reveals himself as a "heavenly Father." In contrast, they vainly worshiped unknown gods and lifeless idols which repeatedly demanded much from them but offered nothing in return.

In his teaching, Jesus introduced his God, who was going to take care of them as the Father does his children. The crowd yearned for, related to, and identified with these lessons. Jesus then exhorted his listeners to seek first the kingdom of God and his righteousness. This kingdom is not a geographical one, but a spiritual realm where his authority and righteousness reigns. As they prioritized these things, Jesus affirmed that all the necessities of life they sought would be given to them. He concluded by telling them not to be anxious about tomorrow because there is always enough stress to deal with today.

Anxiety may be defined as having divided and distracted thoughts. Left unchecked, this invites and amplifies the unwanted emotions of doubt, worry and fear. The remedy to this stress, Jesus taught, was to consider and seek God first, and have a single focus on his care. Jesus concluded his teaching: even though stress may come knocking at the door, God promises to help. His faithful and watchful care is for today, tomorrow and always.[4]

PRACTICING PURPOSEFUL PRAYER

Paul wrote, "Don't worry about anything; instead, pray about everything; tell God your needs, and don't forget to thank him for his answers." Anything means exactly that: anything—and everything! Nothing is to be overlooked as a proposition to pray. There is nothing too big or too small for God. Prayer is how we seek him first. We are also to approach God in prayer with expressions of gratitude. Psalms instructs, "You can pass through his open gates with the password of praise. Come right into his presence with thanksgiving. Come bring your thank offering to him and affectionately bless his beautiful name!" It is impossible to be thankful and unthankful at the same time. When our minds gravitate to ungratefulness, our hearts hop onto the train heading to Unhappyville. There is *always* something for which we can be thankful.[5]

Peter emphasized humility and prayer as solutions to stress as he addressed leaders of the early Christian church. "Indeed all of you should defer to one another and wear the 'overall' of humility in serving each other. 'God resists the proud, but gives grace to the humble. So, humble yourselves under God's strong hand, and in his own good time he will lift you up." The overalls of humility describe the outfit of one who serves others. They are included in the fashionable wardrobe of the new creation in Christ.

I once asked a humble believer from India to define humility. He pondered for a minute, then opened his arms as wide as possible and said in broken English, "God—this big!" Then he closed his arms and held up his thumb and index finger to where they were almost touching. "Me—this little."

The language of humility is portrayed by the imagery of lying down. The benefit of lying down under God's strong hand is we will be lifted up by his personal and timely intervention. I am reminded of a line from the Psalms, "But You, Eternal One, wrap around me like an impenetrable shield. You give me glory and lift my eyes up to the heavens." My mind pictures our heavenly Father, enveloping a humble-hearted child whose head is hung low. Then, with his gentle but immense hands, God tenderly and slowly lifts up the child's chin for an eye-to-eye encounter. Can you imagine experiencing a moment like this, overwhelmed by his awesome and loving care?

How do we humble ourselves in this way before God? Peter reveals the answer. "By casting all your cares on him because he cares for you." To *cast* something is to deliberately throw it. Once we cast our cares and stresses onto God, we are *never* to take them back! We can confidently cast our cares upon him in prayer, knowing we are the object of his care. Like an expert archer carefully aiming to hit the bullseye of a target, God purposefully aims for the bullseye of our hearts, releasing his watchful care, concern and blessings upon each one of us. Remember how big he is and how little we are. There is absolutely no problem he can't handle or any circumstance that catches him off guard.[6]

As I meditated upon overcoming distraction and worry through prayer, I found comfort and peace. I rested in the *God Place*. My long day at the airport came to a close and I resolved to spend the night there. Meanwhile, my wonderful wife sent me the India visa via overnight mail. There was a facility within the airport that offered a napping room and a shower, so I settled in for the night, reveling in God's peace. The next day, after picking up the visa at a nearby cargo terminal, I briskly walked back to the airport with just enough time to check in. Once again my "angel" was on duty behind the counter, and I enjoyed sharing the victory with her by presenting the required original documents for international departure. Her sweet disposition made such an impression upon my heart that I was prompted to ask her what religion she practiced.

Somewhat surprised at my question, she hesitantly divulged, "I don't have a religion."

"You have exhibited more kindness to me than many religious people I know."

She lifted her tear-filled eyes to meet mine, and while trying to maintain her professional composure softly whispered, "Nobody has ever told me anything like that before."

Before I boarded, she secured an exit row seat so I could stretch out my long legs for the ten-hour flight. She also wanted a picture taken with me and gave me her phone number so that I could send the photo to her. Her final act of benevolence was to leave her post behind the counter at the gate to personally escort me down the long jet bridge and to the door of the plane. It was evident she wanted to hug, but because of cultural and professional considerations, we mutually settled for a courteous bow to each other and then a warm handshake. With a final salutation, I turned and boarded the plane.

Throughout the airport adventure and the journey that followed, it became clear that God was pouring out his care on me. Regardless of the circumstances, he was holding my hand the entire time. I recalled an exhortation to Joshua recorded in Deuteronomy. "Be strong. Take courage. Don't be intimidated. Don't give them a second thought because God, your God, is striding ahead of you. He's right there with you. He won't let you down; he won't leave you. Don't be intimidated. Don't worry." Hebrews affirms this promise, "and be content with what you have because He has said, 'I will never leave you; I will always be by your side.'" The Scriptures propound this truth over and over again: "Fear not. I am with you!"[7]

Contentment means focusing on what we *have*, not on what we *don't have*. Deliberately choosing which thoughts to dwell on breeds an attitude of gratitude. Remember: it is impossible to be thankful and unthankful at the same time. When unthankful thoughts flood our minds, we should simply meditate upon everything we are presently thankful for and our hearts will change from restlessness to contentment. This is a cure for discontentment and anxiety.

As I continued my travels over the next month in Africa

and India, two themes reoccurred, unhindered by time, place or circumstance: "God is always with you," and "Look for things to be thankful for in every situation." These messages of promise and comfort sustained me through the remaining days of the trip and provided a victorious outcome. Although I did not tell anyone about the financial burden from the India visa mix-up, unsolicited and abundant finances flooded in to cover the unforeseen expenses. The trip gave me the opportunity to minister in five countries while enjoying health, safety, and an overall prosperous and fruitful journey. Thousands of lives were touched.

ENJOY THE RIDE

Here's another travel story: several years ago, I was flying to a conference when bad weather forced us to land and to stay grounded for the night. All the passengers were put on standby for the first flights out the next morning. I took my place in the back of a long line of irate customers, many of them yelling at the personnel behind the airline counter. When it was my turn, the customer-weary airline representative placed me forty-ninth on the standby list. I complimented her on what a great job she was doing, then opted for a complimentary floor mat in the airport instead of spending money on a nearby hotel. After things settled down, I got up to stretch and again walked over to the frazzled airline personnel behind the counter to offer further words of compassionate appreciation. My desire was to help soothe their souls from the marathon of unnecessary verbal abuse they had just endured.

Returning to my mat, I determined to push aside concerns about whether I'd get to the conference on time the next day. Reaching into my briefcase, I pulled out a biography of George Müller. As I read truths written in 1832, a vital lesson unfolded that I believe is relevant to everyone, especially those in ministry who are caught up in the trap of service, like Martha was, rather than going to their *God Place*.

On April 20th Mr. Müller left for Bristol. On the journey he was dumb, having no liberty in speaking for Christ or even in giving away tracts, and this led him to reflect. He saw that the so-called 'work of the Lord' had tempted him to substitute action for meditation and communion. He had neglected that still hour with God which supplies to spiritual life alike its breath and its bread. No lesson is more important for us to learn, yet how slow are we to learn it: that for the lack of habitual seasons set apart for devout meditation upon the word of God and for prayer, nothing else will compensate. We are prone to think, for example, that converse with Christian brethren, and the general round of Christian activity, especially when we are much busied with preaching the Word and visits to inquiring or needy souls, make up for the loss of aloneness with God in the secret place. We hurry to a public service with but a few minutes of private prayer, allowing precious time to be absorbed in social pleasures, restrained from withdrawing from others by a false delicacy, when to excuse ourselves for needful communion with God and his word would have been perhaps the best witness possible to those whose company was holding us unduly! How often we rush from one public engagement to another without any proper interval for renewing our strength in waiting on the Lord, as though God cared more for the quantity than the quality of our service! Here Mr. Müller had the grace to detect one of the foremost perils of a busy man in this day of insane hurry. He saw that if we are to feed others we must be fed; and that even public and united exercises of praise and prayer can never supply that food which is dealt out to the believer only in the closet—the shut-in place with its closed door and open window, where he meets God alone.[8]

Müller's story teaches us about the need to consistently go to our *God Place*. Sometimes we're so busy *being* busy that we are not paying attention to God. Interestingly, even in the early 1800s, Müller described the times in which he lived as "insane, hurried, busy and rushed." I was amazed while reading his account. *These were the days of the horse and buggy.* I thought. *How could there have been all this hustle and bustle? Wasn't life simpler back then compared to this modern day?* Then I remembered how a century earlier Susanna Wesley, mother of John and Charles Wesley, dealt with the stress of life's routine. She stopped whatever she was doing and pulled her apron over her head. This signified that she had gone to her *God Place* and for her children not to disturb her.

The next morning, as I took an airport monorail to another terminal to see if I could catch a better flight, I noticed a young, anxious couple who appeared to be worried about their flight status. But their small child, oblivious to what was going on, was joyfully singing and skipping around a metal pole. God whispered to my heart, "Just become like a child and enjoy the ride of life. Give me your burdens." Unable to find any better flight, I returned to the original terminal to check on my standby position. The display board still listed me as number forty-nine, but I recalled the child and God's directive to me as anxiety knocked on my mind's door. That's when a particularly angry person, apparently in eighth position, began screaming at the airline personnel, the same attendants who had been there the night before. Unhappy with his standby status, he hollered, "What are you going to do about it?" The airline attendant calmly looked up from her computer screen, glared at him and said, "Watch this!" Faster than the blink of an eye, his name plummeted from number eight to eighty-eight, the very last name on the list. She then glanced over at me, and with a slight smirk moved my name up to take his place in eighth position. In the end, I was the last standby customer permitted to board and made it to the conference on time. Had there been a handrail pole nearby, I would have skipped around it and made a merry melody to the Lord.

GOD'S CARING AND OUR *DOING*

God faithfully promises that he has, he does, and he will personally care for us as a Father for his children. Matthew and Luke both contain a story reassuring us of God's care. Matthew records two sparrows being sold for a farthing, whereas Luke mentions five sparrows sold for two farthings, suggesting that the sparrows were of little value because one was thrown in for free. Yet, as these verses declare, not one sparrow falls to the ground unnoticed, nor are they forgotten by God. The passages continue, reminding us that the very hairs of our heads are numbered. These idioms inform us that whatever may seem trivial to us is of utmost importance to God. He tends to the minutest details of our lives and finds significance in those things we undervalue. Therefore, we are advised to never allow any circumstance to suggest he doesn't care for us, even for a moment. Our true value is declared in Ephesians. "For we are God's masterpiece. He has created us anew in Christ Jesus, so we can do the good things he planned for us long ago." A masterpiece is an outstanding work: rare, one of a kind and even priceless. Just as an art collector devotes conscientious care to each masterpiece, God watches over us with unceasing attention and meticulous detail. God gave us purpose when he created us to be *doers* of good works which he has planned. These include his plans to "prosper you, not to harm you…to give you a future filled with hope."[9]

We learn best from doing. When I attended a prominent cooking school in New York years ago, we were first given three weeks of academic instruction, complete with demonstrations from professional instructors on a particular culinary subject. Immediately following the classroom training, we were thrust into the kitchen to practice what we had just learned. Even though we wore pristine attire and appeared to be polished chefs, our natural abilities came under the spotlight when we were asked to perform the skills acquired from the lectures. Our strengths and weaknesses became evident as we put our acquired knowledge into practice.

I know many people who are in the habit of purchasing the latest self-help books and teaching series, or running to the next conference or seminar which promises to deliver an incredible amount of usable knowledge. Yet with all that input, they still struggle to grow. Why is this? Jesus provides the answer in Matthew and subsequently in Luke. He compares two types of people: one who hears his sayings and does them, and the other who hears his teachings but doesn't do them. The one who hears and does is called a wise person who builds his house upon a rock or solid foundation. The other who hears but does not do is likened to a fool who builds his house on sand or an unstable foundation. Both built a house (a reflection of their lives) and both houses originally stood until stresses came against them. It was then that the foundation determined which house stood against adversity and which one fell. A solid foundation is not built by hearing alone, but by doing, or acting upon, that which is heard. We may have a wealth of knowledge, but unless it is actively applied, our foundation will fail. Simply acknowledging God's truths will not produce change. God's benefits are realized with practicing his promises.

What type of foundation are we building our lives on? Will we be unshakeable when the flood waters rise? Doing is practicing, and practicing truth will produce unconditional blessings and genuine happiness. Jesus shared, "You know these things—now do them! That is the path of blessing." This path of blessing leads to Happyville.

It is in *doing* that we realize the caring presence of God and experience his freedom. James tells us, "But whoever looks intently into the perfect law that gives freedom, and continues in it—not forgetting what they have heard, but doing it—they will be blessed in what they do."[10]

It is always liberating to do something with the knowledge God has given us. As I was working on the initial manuscript of this book, I passed it on to a friend to read. I'll call him Eugene. He was so inspired by this section on "doing" that he wanted to share with me the time he applied this teaching to overcome an unexpected bout with fear and self-doubt. It happened when he took a weeklong business trip three states away from home to conduct marketing training with one of his newest clients. Eugene had done this kind of training before and was well prepared for the five-day, one-on-one coaching session, and for good reason. His new client was affluent and well-connected in his particular profession. Eugene knew that if he could perform and impress this client, a potentially expansive and lucrative market segment could be opened to his business.

Eugene arrived at the client's city with confidence, but the moment he got to the hotel the client reserved for his visit, an intense feeling of intimidation suddenly rose up in him. It was a prestigious hotel and Eugene was appointed a luxurious suite overlooking the metropolis. As Eugene took in the stunning view of the skyscrapers from the picture window of his far-too-large and extravagant room, he thought, *Oh my God. What am I doing here? I'm totally out of my league. I'm not good enough for all of this.* After a decidedly restless night, he met with his client and they completed their first full day of work. But as he left his client's palatial office, Eugene contemplated, *I think that went well. He seemed pleased. Still, I can't help but think everything I said was gibberish. Useless.*

Eugene attempted to console himself by going to a professional baseball game that night, something that always relaxed him, but his anxiety only intensified. Driving on the freeway from the ballpark back to the hotel, he wanted to keep on driving, past the hotel, out of the city and towards home. Back in his room, Eugene felt weak and bewildered. He couldn't open his Bible. He couldn't formally pray. He was overwhelmed. But, as he lay down in his bed, Eugene *did something*. He went to his *God Place*, entering in by uttering one simple word to his heavenly Father: "Help!"

It was all he had—but it was all he needed. As Eugene drifted off into a sound sleep, God gently ministered to his heart and mind. The next morning, Eugene awoke with a renewed vigor and the refreshing realization that a massive weight had been removed from his shoulders. Fear and self-doubt were gone, replaced by an overwhelming sensation of joy and peace. At the close of that day's training session, his client told him, "I just want to thank you for everything we're doing. I couldn't have done any of this on my own. Your insights and guidance have been invaluable to me." My friend thought, *This is so incredible. God really cares for me!* He drove back to the hotel that night singing praises to God and realizing he was "blessed in his doing." Not only was the training successful, the client hired Eugene for additional work and has eagerly referred him to his colleagues.

Just like Eugene, I am convinced that you will discover and realize the purposes and plans that God has for your life. His blessings are born out of his great love and personal care for you. As you apply the teachings from this book, you will wake up each morning and anticipate doing what God sets before you as he personally reveals his perfect will for your day.

Who cares? God cares! This joyful anticipation of looking for the promises of God to unfold in our lives is also called *hope*. We will probe this topic in the next chapter.

References

1.   Luke 10:38-42 (GW)

2.   Colossians 3:15a

3.   Proverbs 3:24 (NAS); Psalm 3:5 (NLT) and Psalm 4:8 (NET)

4.   Referenced from Matthew 6:22-32 and Luke 12:22-32

5.   Philippians 4:6 (TLB) and Psalm 100:4 (TPT)

6.   1 Peter 5:5b-6 (J.B. PHILLIPS); Psalm 3:3 (VOICE) and 1 Peter 5:7 (NET)

7.   Deuteronomy 31:6, 8 (MSG) and Hebrews 13:5b (VOICE)

8.   Pierson, A.T., George Müller of Bristol: (New York: The Baker and Taylor Company, 1899) pp. 94 -95

9.   Matthew 10:29-31; Luke 12:6-7; Ephesians 2:10 (NLT) and Jeremiah 29:11b (NET)

10. Referenced from Matthew 7:24-27; Luke 6:47-49; John 13:17 (TLB) and James 1:25 (NIV)

CHAPTER 15

WHAT DO YOU EXPECT?

Since the fall of humankind, the world has become an unstable place characterized by restlessness. Governments and political systems are tainted with corruption. The cost of living is skyrocketing. Unknown diseases baffle the scientific community. There are economic crashes and banks in need of bailouts. Credit card debt is out of control; identity theft is rampant. School shootings. Teen suicides. Racism. The news media are saturated with negativity. These all fuel a fear of the future, resulting in the substance abuse of alcohol, painkillers and anti-anxiety medications. Yet all of these self-soothing remedies fall short of bringing lasting peace.

There is an increasing concern about the quality of home life. It is deteriorating at an alarming rate. Social media and entertainment are replacing personal communication. Relationships are harder to develop and maintain as promises and commitments are made, but not kept. Churches are losing members by the droves as many hurt and disillusioned attendees witness and experience hypocrisy, unfaithfulness and legalistic control.

People from all walks of life are at the end of their rope. Morale and hope have been crushed. Society's blazing fire of ambition has been reduced to the smoldering embers of apathy.

Despite the intensifying perception of these calamities, God has *not* turned his back on us. The book of Lamentations speaks to our times: "Yet there is one ray of hope: his compassion never ends. It is only the Lord's mercies that have kept us from complete destruction. Great is his faithfulness; his loving-kindness begins afresh each day. My soul claims the Lord as my inheritance; therefore I will hope in him. The Lord is wonderfully good to those who wait for him, to those who seek for him. It is good both to hope and wait quietly for the salvation of the Lord."[1]

God declares that he is love and light. There is absolutely no hint of darkness in him. All his desires and intentions are therefore rooted in his identity: love and light. Recall that he created us in his image. Therefore, it is not wise to re-form him into our image of him, or to fashion him according to whom we perceive him to be. Before believing in Christ, we were separated from God. We were strangers and without hope. But there is good news: because we are one with Christ through his accomplishments for us, we are brought into the inner circle of God's family—with all the rights and privileges as his child. We now have both God *and* hope. We have a steadfastness and certainty about our future so that we can exclaim like the Psalmist, "My life, my every moment, my destiny— it's all in your hands." Isaiah also promises that God is our safety net. He is the stability of our ever-present moment. His treasuries are full of abundance, salvation, wisdom and knowledge. Reverence for his ways is the key that opens the door to his riches and releases heaven's unlimited resources.[2]

Our certainty of God's loving nature determines the degree to which we will trust him with our lives. The epistle of James taught us that God's promises do not vacillate with the circumstances, therefore, neither should we. James also revealed that anyone who is double minded is unstable. That is why we persuade our minds once and for all—God is faithful. When we are convinced of his stability, we will praise him regardless of what is happening around us. No wonder the Scriptures exhort, "Trust God from the bottom of your heart; don't try to figure out everything on your own. Listen for God's voice in everything you do, everywhere you go; he's the one who will keep you on track. Don't assume that you know it all. Run to God! Run from evil! Your body will glow with health; your very bones will vibrate with life!"[3] Holding fast to these truths, that God's love and goodness are real and constant, is the foundation for our rescue from stress.

It is vital to intentionally invite God's life-giving thoughts into our minds and give them the highest priority. As we let them dwell in our hearts, they will become established. It is also imperative to personalize these truths, making them our own until they become as natural as breathing. Going about our day with an underlying uncertainty of God's goodness and love to us is unhealthy. Retaining "iffy" thoughts about him changing his disposition toward us at any given moment generates low but constant levels of stress hormones. This ultimately affects our well-being. As we have already determined, one of the primary objectives of the devil is to attack God's integrity, goodness and love. The primary weapons of destruction in the devil's arsenal include doubt, worry, fear, hopelessness and negative thinking. He hurls endless suggestions at us, accusing God of not forgiving, loving or even liking us. Truth is simple and liberating: God is our Father; we are his children. His goodness and love infinitely surpass any good intentions or expressions of love that we could muster even on our best day!

> *Holding fast to these truths, that God's love and goodness are real and constant, is the foundation for our rescue from stress.*

One of the most amazing advantages of going to our *God Place* is, when any circumstance confronts us, God's presence produces a super-beneficial experience. His outcome is always unparalleled by any other solution. The *God Place* cannot be confined to a location or defined within a set period of time. It may not look the same to everyone, but the door to intimate fellowship in the *God Place* is always open offering comfort, protection, stability and hope.

PERSPECTIVES ON HOPE

There is an immense difference between the way the world recognizes hope and how God defines hope. Some confuse hope with optimism and positive thinking. While those things may be helpful, they lack a firm foundation. The meaning of hope as declared in Scripture is not some unstable, uncertain or wishy-washy expression such as, "I hope I get a raise," or "She hopes it will rain today," or "He's hoping to hear back from them soon." There are no "ifs, buts, or maybes" about it! Genuine hope is a real expectation rooted in a promise that will unfold at an appointed time in the future. It is usually related to a joyful and pleasurable event. The certainty of hope is determined by the guarantor of the promise. When the promise is from God, it overrides and supersedes whatever appears to be contrary to the promise. Even though the promise will be fulfilled in the future, hope in that unseen promise helps sustain patience and guards against the stress that comes from not knowing what lies ahead.

According to Hebrews, faith is trusting in the promises of God. It is the assurance and firm foundation upon which hope rests and proof of the certainty of any unseen promises.[4] Faith does not say, "It appears to be," but exhibits an unshakeable confidence that the future promises of God are a reality and are as good as already accomplished. Hope is the expectation of God's faithful fulfillment to his word before it is evidenced. That is why he is our stability even in our days of distress and times of trouble.

Let's say you buy a new car from a dealer, but it still needs to be delivered. You pay for the car, receive the title, and then wait for the good news that it has arrived at the dealership ready to be picked up. All you need to do is present your title, and you will drive away your brand-new vehicle. The title you presently hold in your hand is proof that the car is coming in the future and fuels your anticipation of its arrival. Similarly, God gives us promises to connect us to what he has already accomplished for us in Christ. Hope prepares our hearts to patiently receive those promises. Hope allows God's promises to define reality rather than our current circumstances. Hope is not just for tomorrow but also extends into eternal life. It is not a *que será, será* (whatever will be, will be) attitude. It requires our participation in determining and receiving favorable results.

We have examined the lives of several people in this book—and they all had hope.

Jacob had hope in the promise that God was going to give him the land upon which he slept. Additionally, all families of the earth would be blessed through his descendants. If that was not enough, God encouraged Jacob by promising to be with him and protect him wherever he went.

God told the prophet Samuel to anoint David as king of Israel when Saul was still the king. David kept this hope throughout his days of running from Saul. Later, David spoke of his own life and prophesied the same words over the coming Messiah. "Therefore my heart is glad and my tongue rejoices; my body also will rest in hope, because you will not abandon me to the realm of the dead, you will not let your holy one see decay."[5]

When Asaph became distraught with his perception of how unbelievers prospered, he went into his *God Place* and the Lord revealed to him the destructive destiny awaiting those who rejected God. This gave Asaph the hope of being guided with God's counsel in his present life and then of being received up to glory afterwards.

When Jehoshaphat was confronted with a hopeless situation, he was strengthened with hope as he reminded the Lord of these promises. God was ruler over all kingdoms and so powerful and mighty that no one could withstand him. Should evil come upon

God's children, they were instructed to stand before the sanctuary, their *God Place*, and in his presence cry out to him knowing he would hear and help them.

Approximately one week before Jesus was crucified, he raised Lazarus back to life. Perhaps God had Jesus raise Lazarus as a way of instilling the hope that he, too, was also going to rise from the grave three days after his crucifixion. This miracle refreshed the remembrance of the prophecy David declared regarding the resurrection and the joy that was to be set before Christ. Our Savior went to and endured the cross with the hope and confidence of the Psalmist's report: "For you bring me a continual revelation of resurrection life, the path to the bliss that brings me face-to-face with you."[6]

Additionally, Abraham was a great example of someone who hoped in the Lord. Encouraged by the God who "calls the things that are not, as though they were," Abraham was given a sign of hope from God. Genesis records, "Then God brought Abram outside beneath the nighttime sky and told him, 'Look up into the heavens and count the stars if you can. Your descendants will be like that—too many to count!'" Later, God confirmed this promise by changing the patriarch's name from Abram (exalted father) to Abraham (father of a multitude of nations). Even when Abraham was childless, God spoke destiny into him. Can you imagine how Abraham's hope was strengthened each time he gazed into the star-filled heavens or when his new name was publicly confessed? That is why Abraham focused on and glorified God—and not his surrounding circumstances. Abraham was fully persuaded of God's faithfulness to carry out what he promised.

The Book of Romans reiterates God's faithfulness. "Abraham, when hope was dead within him, went on hoping in faith, believing that he would become 'the father of many nations.' He relied on the word of God which definitely referred to 'your descendants'. With undaunted faith he looked at the facts—his own impotence (he was practically a hundred years old at the time) and his wife Sarah's apparent barrenness. Yet he refused to allow any distrust of a definite pronouncement of God to make him waver. He drew strength from his faith, and while giving the glory to God, remained absolutely convinced that God was able to implement his own promise." Abraham was old and his wife Sarah was well beyond child bearing age when God affirmed that Abraham was going to be the father of many nations. Yet Abraham found hope in the face of hopelessness and refused to consider the facts presented by his five senses. With unwavering trust, he secured God's promise to him. Abraham's faith grew strong because of his frequent visits to the *God Place*, where he gazed with awe at the stars and reflected on his new name while communing with his Creator.[7]

PAUL: HOLDING ON TO HOPE IN THE MIDST OF ADVERSITY

We have learned that there are different degrees of stress, identified in Scripture as "trouble" and "distress." Stress is a response to an event, condition, experience or other stimuli. Stressors include mental, physical and spiritual causes and stem from both internal and external circumstances. Stress affects everyone. We also know what may seem easy for one person to endure may be difficult for another.

The apostle Paul certainly experienced stress with a frequency and intensity most of us could not likely endure. Paul dealt with people trying to kill him. He was stoned and left for dead. He was severely beaten and imprisoned multiple times. He sustained several shipwrecks—once treading turbulent waters in the open sea for an entire day and night. He labored hard during the day yet endured many cold and sleepless nights, often going hungry and thirsty.

Paul may never have imagined such personal stress was possible before encountering Jesus Christ. Prior to that encounter, Paul, then known as Saul, surely believed he had everything going for him. He came out of the right stock, a Pharisee who enjoyed all the worldly privileges that came with that religious status. He was more zealous than his peers and was a likely candidate for the cover of *The Jerusalem Times Magazine* as "Man of the Year." Like a relentless bloodhound tenaciously tracking the scent of an escaped prisoner, Saul's mission was to find and persecute those who bucked against the religious leaders of the time. He purposed to extinguish the rebellious movement of those who proclaimed a risen Messiah. Saul, the rising religious star, had the reputation of being both revered and feared.

Paul refused to dwell on the temporary things which he could see, but rather focused on those unseen things that endure forever.

After his encounter with the resurrected Christ, a transformation took place and Paul became a loyal follower of the risen Messiah. He soon assessed all of his earthly accolades as "rubbish." When he began his revolutionary ministry, he experienced relentless opposition. This opposition was from certain Jewish religious leaders who were determined to keep others under the law, the Gentiles who wanted to keep worshipping their idolatrous gods, and the false apostles and teachers who boasted in their abilities while slandering Paul and his message of the gospel of Jesus Christ. Part of that gospel pertained to the hope of the return of the Messiah and the eternal life which awaited every believer in Christ. Paul contended against the traditions of both Jewish and Greek philosophers who muddied the understanding of eternal life, ranging from the doctrine of no resurrection from the dead to the rumor that Jesus had already come back, to the hedonistic attitude of "eat, drink, and be merry, for tomorrow we die." He challenged various doctrines on reincarnation, immortality, judgment, heaven and hell which had infiltrated the cultures of his time. Many of these ideologies continue to pervade our modern-day thinking throughout the world.

On top of all that, Paul expressed a compassionate concern for all of the home churches and city-wide fellowships that were suddenly springing up. He traveled to visit some of those churches and fellowships and wrote to others from prison. Paul tirelessly taught God's truths that were revealed to him by the Holy Spirit, and he did all this while being relentlessly bombarded by stress and temptation.

How did Paul endure all of those circumstances? He discovered the treasures of hope in God and taught them to others by demonstrating how they, too, could apply the aspects of hope in their everyday lives while extending it unto their promised eternal life. One gem Paul shared regarded audible confession. He exclaimed, "It is written: 'I believed; therefore I have spoken.' Since we have that same spirit of faith, we also believe and therefore speak, because we know that the one who raised the Lord Jesus from the dead will also raise us with Jesus and present us with you to himself." Speaking what we believe, our confession, causes our ears to hear and resonate those words to our brains where they are further communicated into our hearts. Paul knew what he believed regarding hope in God and spoke it in the face of his adversity. From Paul we learn that our confession of God's promises distresses the devil and his kingdom of darkness.

Another jewel Paul discovered was how to view life's events through the lens of hope. He declared, "For our light affliction, which is but for a moment, is working for us a far more exceeding and eternal weight of glory, while we do not look at the things which are seen, but at the things which are not seen. For the things which are seen are temporary, but the things which are not seen are eternal." The word "affliction" as used here corresponds to the Old Testament Hebrew word frequently translated as *distress*. Paul perceived his stress as light and momentary because he realized that the scales were tipped in his favor by the everlasting weight of God's glory. Therefore, he refused to dwell on the temporary things which he could see, but rather focused on those unseen things that endure forever. He taught these same truths to the Romans. "In my opinion whatever we may have to go through now is less than nothing compared with the magnificent future God has planned for us."[8]

How could Paul say he looked at things that were unseen? His prayer for the Ephesians reveals, "I keep asking that the God of our Lord Jesus Christ, the glorious Father, may give you the Spirit of wisdom and revelation, so that you may know him better. I pray that the eyes of your heart may be enlightened in order that you may know the hope to which he has called you, the riches of his glorious inheritance in his holy people."[9] It takes revelation from God to know him experientially and the calling he has for each of us. He enlightens us to see the unseen with the eyes of our heart. He does this through his Spirit, giving us vivid visions while powerfully inspiring our imaginations. Having this gift of the Holy Spirit is like a title deed to the promises of the future.

Paul described it this way:

In him you also, when you heard the word of truth, the gospel of your salvation, and believed in him, were sealed with the promised Holy Spirit, who is the guarantee of our inheritance until we acquire possession of it, to the praise of his glory. And he has identified us as his own by placing the Holy Spirit in our hearts as the first installment that guarantees everything he has promised us. God is the one who has prepared us for this change, and he gave us his Spirit as the guarantee of all that he has in store for us.[10]

What is God speaking to your heart right now? What are the desires he is showing you? What personal visions is he revealing? As *The Message* Bible says, "If people can't see what God is doing, they stumble all over themselves; But when they attend to what he reveals, they are most blessed." It requires us to pay attention to the present presence of God. This takes practice, but it is well worth it.

Hebrews exhorts, "You always have God's presence. For hasn't he promised you, 'I will never leave you alone, never! And I will not loosen my grip on your life!'" God is always ready to welcome us into the *God Place* and display what he has for us. He also has the vantage point of knowing our whole life ahead of time. He is quite aware of what lies around the corner, and because he is love, he yearns to guide us into enjoying the best life now and throughout all eternity.

This is why hope is such an integral part of walking with God. He announces, "From the beginning I declare how things will end; from times long past, I tell what is yet to be, saying: "My intentions will come to pass. I will make things happen as I determine they should." God has a *personal* plan for each one of us—and that, my friend, is the hope of his calling for your life! Do you recall God's affirmation? "'For I know the plans and thoughts that I have for you,' says the Lord, 'plans for peace and well-being and not for disaster, to give you a future and a hope.'" Godly peace includes favor, prosperity, safety, complete contentment and health.[11]

As we focus on the thoughts and plans which God reveals, we enjoy perfect peace and an assurance of a hopeful future. Isaiah affirms that as our desire rests on God, God himself will preserve us in perfect peace because we trust in him. Young's Literal Translation describes this focus as one's imagination leaning upon and supported by God. Imagination is very powerful. It is the process of forming mental images of something not presently available to the senses. Whoever or whatever influences our imagination influences our destiny. Think of the expression, "making a mountain out of a molehill." It is referring to using the imagination to magnify a small problem into a giant one. What if we exercised our Godly imaginations to magnify his resources, thus minimizing our problems? We will have peace. Picture yourself becoming who you want to be, having what you desire and arriving where you want to go. As you live from the place of your desired destination, your imagination will help lead you there. Take the time to imagine what your *God Place* looks like. Become an

What if we exercised our Godly imaginations to magnify his resources, thus minimizing our problems?

accomplished photographer: survey the area, focus on the beautiful details and shoot the picture, then see what develops.

What wonderful opportunities await those who go to the *God Place* with all their hearts, souls, and minds! This is where God imparts his plans for you. Remember, "For we are God's masterpiece. He has created us anew in Christ Jesus, so we can do the good things he planned for us long ago." Do you want the best possible life now and through all eternity? Allow God to reveal his plans and purposes for you through the Holy Spirit.[12]

NAVIGATING LIFE BY THE SPIRIT OF GOD

Three of my friends who are pilots provided metaphorical insights, illuminating truths of walking with God in light of hope.

Tim, a retired flight instructor, was involved in military combat training. He discussed the importance of flight plans and strategic missions, and explained that the execution of orders given to each fighter aircraft demanded crew interaction, accuracy, precision and timing because the many personnel involved in a mission required a coordinated plan. "If a pilot or crew member was self-willed with their orders," Tim said, "imagine the havoc, confusion and consequences that would ensue." God has a plan for us: we want to seek his perspective, wisdom and plan for our lives. It, too, involves interacting with others (divine appointments), necessitating exactness, veracity and prearranged coordination.

He went on to describe a valuable flight instrument called the *attitude indicator*, which displays the orientation of an aircraft relative to the earth's horizon. "It is crucial to staying on the right path and moving toward the destination," he explained. Our attitude regarding God informs us of our orientation to his plan for us. Jesus shared, "Whatever is in the heart overflows into speech." No wonder we are instructed, "So above all, guard the affections of your heart, for they affect all that you are. Pay attention to the welfare of your innermost being, for from there flows the wellspring of life."[13]

Earlier in the book, the concept of *entertaining a thought* was introduced. It depicts inviting thoughts into the home of our hearts and making them comfortable. When it comes to the ideas and notions that knock on our mind's door, we are to be like a sentry who demands, "Who goes there?" Why is this important? As we change what we think about, it changes our confession—and changes our destiny! As a believer in Christ, our mission in life is really a commission (a "co-mission"), because God is our partner. Recall that God is presently and continually working in us. Our passion for his influential involvement indicates how well we are staying on the right path and moving toward the destination he has preplanned for us.

Joe, the second aviator, is a longtime friend who graduated from the U.S. Naval Academy and served as a helicopter pilot. Part of his role included search and rescue operations. During his active duty he repeatedly witnessed new flight school students boasting in their abilities—that is, until they were initially taken up in a helicopter as passengers and blinded with hoods over their heads. As the pilot maneuvered the helicopter, the students were required to guess the orientation of the aircraft. Was it ascending or descending, or was it banking to the left or right? Many times, they were surprised as their hoods were removed. Their senses convinced them that they were ascending to the right, when in fact they were descending to the left. Joe explained this phenomenon as "spatial disorientation," the inability of a pilot to correctly interpret the aircraft's attitude, altitude or airspeed in relation to other points of reference.

The student pilots were quickly humbled as they realized they couldn't trust their senses. Fatal crashes have occurred when pilots thought they were moving in the right direction, but their senses deceived them. "Trust only in your instruments. They won't deceive you!" That's the non-negotiable command drilled into student pilots. It's especially necessary in search and rescue missions where storms and darkness impede the senses of the pilot. Even after new pilots begin to fly, their instructors randomly pull fuses on some of the flight instruments to determine whether or not the pilot is paying attention to them.

The Spirit of God is much like those instruments. We become disoriented in life when we trust in our five senses. Joe likens it to God saying, "Trust in my Spirit." The fruit of the Spirit are like the instruments in the cockpit. They indicate whether you are on course and moving in the right direction. As Paul wrote in Galatians, "But the fruit produced by the Holy Spirit within you is divine love in all its varied expressions: joy that overflows, peace that subdues, patience that endures, kindness in action, a life full of virtue, faith that prevails, gentleness of heart, and strength of spirit." These are the indicators, the flight instruments that display our true orientation and trajectory along our journey with him through life. We allow God's Spirit to help us navigate the ups and downs of life, but we must be attentive because our free will determines how well we pay attention to his leading. "Now since we have chosen to walk with the Spirit, let's keep each step in perfect sync with God's Spirit."[14]

The last of my pilot friends, Charlie, flew cargo planes with the U.S. Air Force. He shared about the importance of air traffic control, explaining that the tower knows the flight plan of each aircraft and coordinates its position both on the ground and in the air. After an aircraft takes off from the runway, it is handed off to different air traffic personnel who monitor the aircraft and provide guidance for a safe flight from departure to arrival. This includes communicating with the pilot whether the aircraft is heading off course, into a danger zone or approaching a threatening weather pattern. Constant communication with the control tower helps the flight crew know where they have been, where they are, where they are going and how to get there.

The apostle Paul wrote in his letter to the Philippians, "I don't depend on my own strength to accomplish this; however I do have one compelling focus: I forget all of the past as I fasten my heart to the future instead."[15] Paul did not dwell on his past, including any regrets or accolades pertaining to his Jewish background or even the dynamics of his new life in Christ to that point. Paul realized God was involved in his past yet lived in each present moment with unveiled hope for the future. The Book of Revelation declares of God, "I am Alpha and Omega, the beginning and the ending, saith the Lord, which is, and which was, and which is to come, the Almighty."[16] Today is yesterday's future and tomorrow's past. Sometimes our minds swing like a pendulum from harping on the past to assuming a dim-lit future. Our new life in Christ appreciates each present moment, because God dwells in the eternal now.

The fruit of the Spirit are like the instruments in the cockpit. They indicate whether you are on course and moving in the right direction.

Just like air traffic controllers know the position of a flight from its origin to its destination, God knows where we have been, where we are presently and where we are heading. With his help, we can focus on our journey by viewing our past with a thankful remembrance of where he has brought us, while continually recognizing his present presence and by looking for his future direction. This includes the details of when, where and how to move ahead into his high calling and destiny for our lives.

If God ever revealed all the details of our lives at once, our brains would sizzle. Instead, he simply makes known our next assignment, and then the next, all in order, unveiling our purpose. Charlie referred to these sequences as waypoints. We deal with waypoints often, whether it is looking for a landmark to identify a place along a hiking trail or relying on our GPS to inform us when and where to turn. In aviation, a waypoint is a navigational reference used to identify the aircraft's current location and indicate a change in direction, speed or altitude along the desired route. Look for the waypoints God is placing before you. Paul articulates in Romans. "How could you not know that His kindness is guiding our hearts to turn away from distractions and habitual sin to walk a new path?"[17] Our hearts respond to kindness as our guide, not stress.

Most people elect to go through life by allowing circumstances to navigate their decisions. It is like "flying by the seat of your pants," a meaning which originated from the force an aviator feels in the pilot's chair while the aircraft is climbing, diving or rotating. Just as pilots developed this intuition prior to the invention of flight and navigational instruments, we intuitively lived by our senses, with our soul sitting in the pilot chair. Now that we have received the gift of the Holy Spirit, our direction comes from a greater source than our five senses. As recorded in Galatians, "Since we are living by the Spirit, let us follow the Spirit's leading in every part of our lives."[18]

Living by the Spirit assures us of a stable and peaceful journey upon earth. The benefits of being a child of God extend into everlasting life. He wants us to be comforted in the certainty of eternity. The return of Jesus Christ is the greatest hope known to humankind. It is the ultimate rescue from stress. Our closing chapter will briefly touch on this topic and communicate more wonderful truths filled with hope.

References

1.   Lamentations 3:21-26 (TLB)

2.   Referenced from Ephesians 2:12; Psalm 31:15a (TPT) and Isaiah 33:6

3.   Proverbs 3:5-7 (MSG)

4.   Referenced from Hebrews 11:1

5.   Acts 2:26 and 27 (NIV)

6.   Psalm 16:11 (TPT)

7.   Romans 4:17b (WEB); Genesis 15:5 (TLB) and Romans 4:18-21 (J.B. PHILLIPS)

8. 2 Corinthians 4:13 and 14 (NIV); 2 Corinthians 4:17 and 18 and Romans 8:18 (J.B. PHILLIPS)

9. Ephesians 1:17 and 18 (NIV)

10. Ephesians 1:13 and 14 (ESV); 2 Corinthians 1:22 (NLT) and 2 Corinthians 5:5 (GNT)

11. Proverbs 29:18 (MSG); Hebrews 13:5b (TPT); Isaiah 46:10 (VOICE) and Jeremiah 29:11 (AMP)

12. Reference taken from Isaiah 26:3 (YLT) and Ephesians 2:10 (NLT)

13. Luke 6:45b (TLB) and Proverbs 4:23 (TPT)

14. Galatians 5:22-23a (TPT) and Galatians 5:25 (VOICE)

15. Philippians 3:13 (TPT)

16. Revelation 1:8

17. Romans 2:4b (VOICE)

18. Galatians 5:25 (VOICE)

CHAPTER 16

OUR RESCUE FROM STRESS - THE RETURN OF JESUS CHRIST

꙳꙳꙳

One cold, rainy night in Limerick, Ireland, my friend Ellen was walking home when a car came speeding out of nowhere and struck her. She was seriously injured. Her hand was fractured; her right foot severed, dangling from her contorted leg. Before the ambulance rushed her to the hospital, Ellen's husband John asked her what she wanted. She replied that she wanted God to heal her impaired body, so John prayed for her healing in the name of Jesus Christ.

After X-rays and surgery, the prospect of Ellen ever walking again seemed impossible. The impending threat of amputation loomed over her. The medical personnel informed her that at best, her only hope was to expect a lifetime of limping. Then one night in the hospital, Ellen saw a vision of Jesus taking off his right leg and giving it to her. From that moment on, she began to imagine walking through the campus of the local university, and seeing the beautiful daffodils that blossomed each spring. She even pictured herself someday running on the beach.

As Ellen continued to pursue her healing from God she was introduced to the book, *The Brain That Changes Itself*, by Norman Doidge, M.D. This book led her to the concept of the "mirror box" (invented by Vilayanur S. Ramachandran, M.D. PhD). The therapy of a mirror box persuades the brain to produce neurological impulses in association with an injured limb by reflecting the image of the opposite limb onto a mirror. By placing the injured limb behind a mirror, the reflected image of the functioning limb appears, sending an illusionary signal to the brain that the injured limb is functioning.

Devising her own mirror box, Ellen further visualized her wholeness. She recalled a quote from Albert Einstein: "The true sign of intelligence is not knowledge but imagination." These resources were revealed to Ellen as she went to her *God Place* for answers. God prescribed a personal path of wisdom which was illuminated with hope. Two or three times each week Ellen had appointments at the clinic where staff attempted to remove lifeless tissue. She later found out her lower leg had developed gangrene, increasing the possibility of amputation. At first the doctors withheld this information from her because they knew she was a believer and didn't want to diminish her hope. (Remember, when God gives you a vision, it's your vision. Others cannot see what you see, therefore do not allow anyone or anything to steal your personal intervention from God.) Three weeks after Ellen's accident, her mother died. Ellen was unable to fly back to the United States for her mother's funeral. But instead of being overwhelmed by grief and despair, Ellen found herself wrapped in supernatural love and peace. Although she had never been brought so low, she was more aware than ever before that the Lord was carrying her in his arms.

She discovered that the flame of hope shines brightest in the darkest night of despair.

Through times of discouragement, Ellen held on tightly to her vision and her confession that she was going to walk, even run, again. She discovered that the flame of hope shines brightest in the darkest night of despair. Although her mind sometimes drifted into the past, recalling the night of the accident, or fast-forwarded to the "what ifs" of the future, God tenderly brought her back to the present and reminded her of the reality of his love, goodness and healing grace.

She had to choose whether to focus on the intimidating thought of losing her leg, or on the potential of her healing deliverance from God. The battle in her mind intensified and then confronted her to make a decision—either bow down to discouragement and defeat or rise up to hope and victory.

Despite the doctor's prognosis and the probability of permanent and crippling nerve damage, Ellen's dreams of walking through the campus to enjoy the daffodils and running on the beach came to pass! Today only a fading scar remains. "Vision and imagination can be infected by fear," Ellen said, "so submit all your fears to God. He is our teacher. What are you going to settle for, a day-to-day existence or the more abundant life? What do you expect? Do you believe that God really means what he says? He truly is both willing and able to do the impossible. You set the bar! You determine the outcome."

THE DIFFERENCE BETWEEN RELIGION AND GOD'S TRUE NATURE

While religion uses fear to try to change human behavior, the true nature of God uses faith, hope and love, transforming the inward person. These three virtues are vital to hold onto like a multi-stranded rope. Why? Because uncertainty breeds uneasiness, especially fear of the future—and fearfulness invites stress. For example, consider this story from an event that took place not long ago:

A pastor of a megachurch held a conference in a huge auditorium with a vast number of attendees both from his congregation and others from around the country. He opened the conference by asking the multitude to close their eyes and honestly ponder the question, "How many of you are afraid of the Rapture?" (The term "Rapture" is an expression originating from a Middle French term meaning, *to carry away*. The Rapture is used in some theological circles, referring to the gathering together of the Body of Christ.)

A hush came over the auditorium as they considered his question. "If you are," he continued, "I want you to raise your hands." To his astonishment, even though the crowd was filled with seasoned churchgoers, leaders and pastors, almost every hand in the auditorium went up!

As they discussed the topic during the conference, they realized they had been subtly duped by certain man-made religious traditions that crept into their thinking and veered them from the truth. They wondered, *How could a loving and gracious God be reduced from a Father and friend to an unpredictable and never satisfied Deity who demanded proof of their love and loyalty? How could he say we are righteous and then make us jump through hoops to receive his blessings? One moment he promises to never leave us or forsake us, and the next he turns his back on us and ignores our prayers? Does he really love us or even like us? Is there any escape from his judgment and wrath?*

The people attending the conference realized they had been afraid to challenge and confront their religious roots, traditions and upbringings. There were so many contradicting concepts causing confusion, it was no wonder they were intimidated about the return of Christ. As they unpacked their past experiences, common patterns emerged. Bible study had somehow replaced relationship with God, and the more they craved knowing God's heart, the more they were advised to participate in yet another religious class, seminar or conference.

As the close of the event drew near, they cried out to God for purpose, relationship, response and love. Their conclusion? They began to realize that such fears, especially of death—or even the Rapture— were unwarranted for believers. Hebrews explains, "Since the children are made of flesh and blood, it's logical that the Savior took on flesh and blood in order to rescue them by his death. By embracing death, taking it into himself, he destroyed the devil's hold on death and freed all who cower through life, scared to death of death."[1]

Our lives on earth are short. The older we get, the more we realize how quickly time passes. There comes a point where we ask the *big* questions: What is my purpose in life? What happens when I draw my last breath? God's perspective of human life on earth is described in the Scriptures. Our days are compared to the flowers of a meadow. They flourish at first and then fade and wither with time. When the seasonal winds blow, they are suddenly whisked away and remembered no more. None of us can foresee the future. Our lives are likened to a vapor that appears for a little while and then like a fleeting shadow, vanishes into nothing.[2]

That is why it's comforting to look beyond our earthly lives to the greatest hope—Christ's second coming. There are two parts to his return. First, Jesus will come in the heavens *for* believers who will be taken from the earth to meet him in the air and then be taken to heaven. Later, Jesus will come to earth *with* the believers, and certain events prophesied in the Old Testament, the four Gospels and the Book of Revelation will be fulfilled.

Regarding the first part of the Lord Jesus Christ's second coming, Paul wrote the believers in Thessalonica emphasizing he did not want them to be uninformed about those believers in Christ who had already died. They were not to grieve like others "who had no hope." Paul explained that Christ was going to descend from heaven someday with the shout of an archangel and the sound of the trumpet of God. At that moment, as recorded in First Thessalonians, "the believers who have died will rise from their graves. Then, together with them, we who are still alive and remain on the earth will be caught up in the clouds to meet the Lord in the air. Then we will be with the Lord forever. So encourage each other with these words."

> *It's comforting to look beyond our earthly lives to the greatest hope—Christ's second coming.*

While the resurrection of the dead had been revealed in the Old Testament and later reiterated by Jesus, the First Epistle to the Corinthians disclosed a secret not previously known: not all believers were going to die, but at Christ's return "those who have died will be raised to live forever. And we who are living will also be transformed. For our dying bodies must be transformed into bodies that will never die; our mortal bodies must be transformed into immortal bodies." All believers are going to be completely changed! Paul's letter to the Philippians also shares about the second coming of Christ and how he "will transform our humble bodies and transfigure us into the identical likeness of his glorified body. And using his matchless power, he continually subdues everything to himself." Finally, John later elaborated, "And that's only the beginning. Who knows how we'll end up! What we know is that when Christ is openly revealed, we will see him—and in seeing him, become like him. All of us who look forward to his coming stay ready, with the glistening purity of Jesus' life as a model for our own."[3]

Clearly, the hope of Christ's return is something for the believer to joyously look forward to and not dread. It is the gospel, the good news! This wonderful hope provides inspiration for us to walk in a godly manner that flows out of God's encouraging goodness and love. He never uses fear or causes despair as means to motivate change. Believers in Christ will be saved from the day of wrath, a season also referred to in Scripture as the "Day of the Lord," where God's judgment and vengeance will be executed with a great tribulation (distress) upon the inhabitants of the earth. Believers will have already been gathered together with our Lord Jesus Christ before those events commence.

At Christ's return many incredible benefits will be fulfilled for the believer. These blessings include: everlasting life, an inheritance as heirs of God and joint heirs with Jesus Christ, rewards and crowns, and no more tears, sorrow or pain. We are saved by God's grace through faith and not by our works, yet Paul wrote to the

Corinthians, "The foundation is laid already, and no one can lay another, for it is Jesus Christ himself. But any man who builds on the foundation using as his material gold, silver, precious stones, wood, hay or stubble, must know that each man's work will one day be shown for what it is. The day will show it plainly enough, for the day will arise in a blaze of fire, and that fire will prove the nature of each man's work. If the work that the man has built upon the foundation will stand this test, he will be rewarded. But if a man's work be destroyed under the test, he loses it all. He personally will be safe, though rather like a man rescued from a fire." Second Corinthians adds, "For one day we will all be openly revealed before Christ on his throne so that each of us will be duly recompensed for our actions done in life, whether good or worthless." After Jesus comes for believers, but before he returns to earth with them, there will be rewards and crowns given in accordance with how we lived our lives and walked in the good works God foreordained us to carry out.

Until then, our Lord Jesus Christ wants us to abide in him and maximize the blessings he has provided us in this life with a greater view toward eternal blessings. He does not want us to suffer any loss, be embarrassed or feel regretful because of the benefits we could have enjoyed throughout all eternity. Therefore, we are exhorted to purify ourselves as he is pure, fully persuaded by the hopeful anticipation of receiving these good things.

The Scriptures clearly reveal that God's heart for us is to allow his Spirit to purify us now and help us achieve a glorious eternity. We are to be comforted and encouraged by the certainty of his grace, rather than discouraged with the uncertainty of the future or its distressful consequences. As we abide in Christ, we will have confidence when we appear before him. Then, when paradise is restored back to God's original intent for his creation with the new heaven and new earth, we will forever live with the Lord—eternally in the *God Place!*[4]

THE HOPE OF SALVATION AND
ANCHOR OF OUR SOULS

The new believers of the first century were taught the truth of this hope and meditated upon it, embedding in their hearts the reality that Christ could return at any moment. Paul also wrote to them about the helmet of salvation or of wearing the hope of salvation as a helmet. My friend Jan Magiera, an author, a student of Aramaic (the language Jesus spoke) and a researcher of the cultural customs of the Bible, says the helmet is representative of two things. One is identification. Head coverings all over the world identify religion, nationality, profession, rank and status. The believer's head covering is to be their identification of salvation and redemption. The other function of the helmet is to protect the head, and more specifically in the context of Paul's teaching, our thoughts. Interestingly, the Aramaic word for hope, in its simplest form, means *to think*. This kind of hope is not only focused on eternal life, but also on living in hope each day. Paul wrote about God's deliverance during stressful times for both his travel companions and himself, "who delivered us out of so great a death, and does deliver; on whom we have set our hope that he will also still deliver us," Jan explains that to the Eastern mind, deliverance is understood in terms of past, present and future. The fullness of our redemption and salvation is already accomplished, is revealed to us daily, and will be fully realized at the return of Christ. This helmet—this kind of hopeful thinking is to be embraced by every believer. It identifies us as those who have been saved and bought with a price. Our thoughts are to daily lead us toward the progressive reality of the hope of our deliverance and the fullness of our salvation.

Even more, the writer of the book of Hebrews used a fantastic image to describe hope. "This certain hope of being saved is a strong and trustworthy anchor for our souls, connecting us with God himself behind the sacred curtains of heaven." An anchor is only functional if it is attached to a stable object. The context of the rest of Hebrews chapter 6 explains that hope is forged by God's faithfulness to his promises. His counsel and oath cannot be changed. This demonstrated his stability, integrity, strength and trustworthiness. Anyone who held fast to this anchor was assured of their safety. In order to grip the anchor of hope, we need to let go of whatever else we are grasping.[5]

During biblical times different kinds of ships used different kinds of anchors, and each anchor had a specific purpose. Most anchors were primarily used for stability: they prevented the boat from drifting or getting off course. This function was especially important during stormy weather and raging seas. By holding fast to the anchor of hope we will experience a steadiness of purpose, a stability that ranges from the subtle change in the currents of distraction in the everyday moment to the most threatening storms of life. Anchors were also lowered onto smaller vessels and used to guide and tow a larger boat into the safety of the harbor, avoiding rocks, sandbars and shallow waters. With hope as the anchor of our souls, our lives are assured both stability and direction. Our anchor is attached to Christ in the very presence of God! Paul reminds us in Ephesians (also echoed in Hebrews) of our past, present and future reality with God because of our oneness in Christ. "For he raised us from the dead along with Christ and seated us with him in the heavenly realms because we are united with Christ Jesus. So God can point to us in all future ages as examples of the incredible wealth of his grace and kindness toward us, as shown in all he has done for us who are united with Christ Jesus" We are anchored to (and therefore live from) this place of authority with a joyful expectation of our future.

Finally, Peter also declared, "Celebrate with praises the God and Father of our Lord Jesus Christ, who has shown us his extravagant mercy. For his fountain of mercy has given us a new life—we are reborn to experience a living, energetic hope through the resurrection of Jesus Christ from the dead. We are reborn into a perfect inheritance that can never perish, never be defiled, and never diminish. It is promised and preserved forever in the heavenly realm for you!" J. B. Phillips translates this passage, "Thank God, the God and Father of our Lord Jesus Christ, that in his great mercy we men have been born again into a life full of hope, through Christ's rising again from the dead! You can now hope for a perfect inheritance beyond the reach of change and decay, 'reserved' in Heaven for you. And in the meantime, you are guarded by the power of God operating through your faith, till you enter fully into the salvation which is all ready for the dénouement of the last day." "Dénouement" simply means *a climax or grand finale.*

Because God raised Jesus from the dead, we have something tangible to hold onto. It is both alive, and stable. An anchor is unseen in the depths of the water, but it makes a big difference! Our anchor of hope is not visible in the heavens, yet we discover the reality of its presence more and more and day by day.[6]

STAYING STEADFAST IN HOPE

God's will and purpose is for us to experience a fulfilling life now and more importantly throughout eternity. Our earthly lives are only a drop in the ocean compared to the realization that we are going to live forever. That is why Jesus announced, "I came that they may have and enjoy life, and have it in abundance [to the full, till it overflows]." *The Message* Bible renders this verse, "I came so they can have real and eternal life, more and better life than they ever dreamed of." God passionately desires a close Father-to-child relationship with us. He longs to give us his very best, eternally. That is why he invites us to enter into a partnership with him in every circumstance. If we accept this relationship, we will maximize our benefits in this life and throughout eternity. The Gospel of John says, "Eternal life means to know and experience you as the only true God, and to know and experience Jesus Christ, as the Son whom you have sent."

This "knowing" is intimate and relational.[7]

Staying on this hope-filled path requires steadfast focus. As we invite and involve both God the father and his son Jesus Christ into our lives, we experience this more abundant life. If we approach passively, we will be influenced by wordly currents and subtly drift away from God. Getting off course is rarely a deliberate act. We suddenly wake up one day and say to ourselves, "*How did we get here?*"

Such steadfast hope is especially vital when dealing with unexpected adversity. Ephesians encourages us, "Never doubt God's mighty power to work in you and accomplish all this. He will achieve infinitely more than your greatest request, your most unbelievable dream, and exceed your wildest imagination! He will outdo them all, for his miraculous power constantly energizes you."[8] Our hope for daily victorious living, filled with a view and joyful anticipation of the imminent return of Christ, is only realized through our relationship with God our Father and the Lord Jesus Christ.

"Now may God, the inspiration and fountain of hope, fill you to overflowing with uncontainable joy and perfect peace as you trust in him. And may the power of the Holy Spirit continually surround your life with his super-abundance until you radiate with hope!"[9]

References

1. Hebrews 2:14 and 15 (MSG)

2. Referenced from Psalm 103:15 and 16; James 4:14 and 1 Peter 1:24

3. 1 Thessalonians 4:16b-18 (NLT); 1 Corinthians 15:52b-53 (NLT); Philippians 3:21 (TPT) and 1 John 3:2a-3 (MSG)

4. Referenced from Romans 5:9; 1 Thessalonians 1:10; 1 Thessalonians 5:9; John 3:16; 2 Thessalonians 2:16; Titus 3:7; 1 John 5:1-13; Romans 8:17; Colossians 3:24; 1 Peter 1:4; 1 Corinthians 3:14; 2 Corinthians 5:9-10; 2 John 8; 1 Corinthians 9:25; 1 Thessalonians 2:19; 2 Timothy 4:8; 1 Peter 5:4; Revelation 21:4; 1 Corinthians 3:11-15 (J.B. PHILLIPS); 2 Corinthians 5:10 (TPT) and 1 John 3:3

5. Ephesians 6:17; 1 Thessalonians 5:8; 2 Corinthians 1:10 (WEB); Magiera, Janet M., The Armor of Victory: (San Diego: LWM Publications, 2017) pp.91-93; and Hebrews 6:19 (TLB)

6.   Ephesians 2:6 and 7 (NLT) and 1 Peter 1:3 and 4 (TPT, J.B. PHILLIPS)

7.   John 10:10b (AMP, MSG) and John 17:3 (MSG)

8.   Ephesians 3:20 (TPT)

9.   Romans 15:13 (TPT)

SOME PARTING THOUGHTS

Before Jesus was crucified, he left some parting thoughts with his followers. "Truly, truly I say to you, whoever believes in me, these works that I do, he also will do and more than these will he do, because I go to the Father. And whatever you ask in my name, I will do for you, so that the Father will be glorified by his Son."[1] This invitation is still extended today: Whoever believes in Jesus will do the same works and more works than he did (indicating quantity, not quality). During his earthly ministry, Christ was limited to one place at one time, but today he lives in the hearts of believers through the Spirit, the "whoevers" like you and me. Now he can manifest his life simultaneously through multiple people, cultures, geographical locations, and times zones. Because he has given each believer his authoritative name, his works continue to be displayed throughout history and around the world. One great work of Jesus was to pray for those who were going to believe in him. "I am not praying for these alone but also for the future believers who will come to me because of the testimony of these."[2] That prayer also includes the "whoevers" of today. And what is the testimony? It's the declaration from Romans; "that if you will confess with your mouth that Jesus is Lord, and believe in your heart that God raised him from the dead, you will be saved."[3]

The familiar verse, John 3:16, pops up all over the world—from notecards to graffiti on bridges to sports arenas and even under the eyes of athletes. One of those athletes, Tim Tebow, was interviewed on Harry Connick Jr.'s television program in December 2016. Tebow described:

"We were playing for the college football national championship on January 8, 2009. I decided to wear John 3:16 under my eyes. During the game, 93 million people decided to Google John 3:16, and it was a pretty cool moment." That's more people than the highest number that ever viewed a televised Billy Graham crusade. Tebow continued, "Exactly three years later, we happened to be playing the Pittsburgh Steelers in the first round of the playoffs when I was with the Denver Broncos—and I didn't know at the time it was exactly three years later. It was January 8, 2012. I just went out there and tried to do whatever I could to win a playoff game."

After his team won the game, Tebow was on his way to the postgame press conference and the Broncos public relations manager excitably approached him.

"Do you realize what just happened?" he asked Tebow.

"Yeah, we just beat the Steelers and we're going to play the Patriots," Tebow casually replied.

"No! Do you realize what happened?" the PR manager asked again, hardly able to contain himself. "It's exactly three years from the day you wore John 3:16 under your eyes. During the game, you threw for 316 yards. Your yards-per-rush were 3.16. Your yards per completion were 31.6, and the Steelers' time of possession was 31:06."

Tebow's concluding comment was, "A lot of people will say it's a coincidence, but I say, 'Big God.'" To top it off, at the moment Tebow threw the game-winning 80-yard touchdown pass—then the NFL's longest postseason pass in overtime history—CBS's final quarter-hour overnight ratings were, yes, a 31.6.

"For God so loved the world, that he gave his only Son, that whoever believes in him should not perish but have eternal life."[4] We the "whoevers," are invited to this more abundant life, but remember:

While God does a lot of inviting, he never oversteps our freedom of will. An unknown writer who quoted from the King James Version of John 3:16 elaborated:

"God"…The greatest Lover,

"So loved"…The greatest degree,

"The world"…The greatest number,

"That He gave"…The greatest act,

"His only begotten Son"…The greatest gift,

"That whosoever"…The greatest invitation,

"Believeth"….The greatest simplicity,

"In Him"…The greatest Person,

"Should not perish"…The greatest deliverance,

"But"….The greatest difference,

"Have"….The greatest certainty,

"Everlasting Life"…The greatest possession.

Jesus is the only one God raised up from the dead never to die again. God made Jesus both Lord and Christ.[5] Many religions teach and practice truths from God; people in ancient cultures were helping their neighbor's oxen out of the ditch long before Jesus declared that truth. But, as the Scriptures declare, only believing in Jesus Christ guarantees salvation and eternal life. True Christianity is not a religion, nor does it consist of what a person does or does not do. Rather, it is what God has done through Christ so that each "whoever" may be reconciled back to him. It is the life and relationship of a loving

Father with his children. And this relationship blossoms through the promise of John 3:16. No religion offers this!

In the Western world, many call themselves Christians, or are at least assumed to be by others. This is common in many countries where the native citizens are born into a religion and therefore considered to be Hindus, Muslims, Jews, Buddhists and so on. Yet today's so-called institutional Christian churches and organizations have unbelievers who regularly attend but are not getting the answer to their question, "What must I do to be saved?" They are not born again! On the other hand, I personally am aware of Hindus, Muslims, Jews, and Buddhists who have confessed Jesus as Lord and are born again believers. However, if you ask them to name their religion, they will respond, "I am Hindu, Muslim, Jewish, Buddhist," whatever it may be, because of cultural influences. For example, even after the apostle Paul and others were saved, they still referred to themselves and were identified by others as Jews.[6]

We must understand that the Christian church is not confined to a building, denomination, organizational structure, or institution. It is a new assembly of those who accepted the invitation of salvation and is made up of Jews and Gentiles (non-Jews) who believe on and are united in the Lord Jesus Christ. This invitation is according to God's purpose and grace in Christ Jesus. His purpose is for believers to be conformed to the image of his firstborn Son, Jesus Christ. The Christian church is also referred to as the body of Christ with Jesus being the head of the body. Christ fills all in all, that is, all things in all members of his body. We are complete in him. No member gets any more than another, for God shows no partiality.[7]

Here's one final story. When Jesus learned that John the Baptist, his cousin, had been beheaded, he could have fallen apart emotionally and been overwhelmed with stress. But he decided to depart to a desert place with his apostles. The harmonious records of this story, found in all four Gospels, reveal that even though Jesus anticipated solitary rest with his apostles, a great multitude followed them into the wilderness. Christ could have had a meltdown because of his grief, but instead he felt compassion for the people. He healed the sick and began to teach all of them many things. As evening approached, the apostles came to Jesus suggesting he send them away to the villages to buy food and find lodging. Christ, however, replied that the multitudes did not need to depart and told his disciples to feed them. Using their own logic, they asked Jesus if they should go to town and buy food. Instead, Jesus told them to assess how much food they had on hand. They reported back that they only had five barley loaves and two small fish. The apostles looked at the multitude and resolved that their resources came up way too short of what was needed to feed them. It looked like an impossible situation.

Jesus, however, did not focus on what they didn't have, but asked the apostles to bring the meager quantity of bread and fish to him. He took that little amount, looked up to heaven, then blessed and gave thanks for what they had. He spoke good over it, invoked blessings and prosperity from above, and thanked God for provision to take care of the people. Next, Jesus had the disciples distribute the loaves and fish to the multitude—and about five thousand men (plus women and children) were *all* satisfied! When they gathered up what remained, the leftovers filled twelve baskets. Abundance!

Be like Jesus: when overwhelming challenges and seemingly impossible moments confront you, don't lean upon your own logic to figure things out. Don't focus on what you *don't* have, but on what you *do* have. Take it, look up to heaven, and speak blessings and prosperity over it in the name of Jesus Christ. God's eyes and ears are always open, searching and listening for a "whoever" to look up and seek him. This is the *God Place*, where our eyes meet his gentle and affectionate glance, and our voices are heard as they enter his attentive ears and saturate his responsive heart. Let's look to him with great expectation and receive our miracle from the *God Place*.

As we conclude our journey together, I pray that you have learned (and will apply) as much from reading this book as I have from writing it. This epilogue, *Some Parting Thoughts*, will be just that for some, yet I truly believe that for others our paths may cross someday, either in person or through some other means of communication.

In the name of Jesus Christ, I pray for you—the "whoever."

This is the God Place, where our eyes meet his gentle and affectionate glance, and our voices are heard as they enter his attentive ears and saturate his responsive heart.

Whether you are contemplating this marvelous journey for the very first time and decide to believe on the Lord Jesus Christ; are just starting down the newfound path as a believer freshly reconciled (connected) to God; perhaps have wandered away from him but are now renewed with fresh determination to reconnect; or even are among those seasoned sons and daughters of God who have walked with him for a long time yet discovering there is more—much, much more; my prayer for you is:

The Lord bless you and keep you; the Lord make his face to shine upon you and be gracious to you; the Lord lift up his countenance upon you and give you peace.[8]

And now I commend you to the care of God and to the message of his grace, which is able to build you up and give you the blessings God has for all his people.[9]

References

1. John 14:12-13 (APNT)
2. John 17:20 (TLB)
3. Romans 10:9 (WEB)
4. John 3:16 (ESV) Taken from Acts 2:36
5. Taken from Acts 16:1, 20 and Acts 22:3
6. Taken from 2 Timothy 1:9; Romans 8:29; Ephesians 1:2; Ephesians 1:23; Colossians 2:10 and

Acts 10:34

7.   Matthew 14:13-21; Mark 6:30-44; Luke 9:10-17 and John 6:1-15

8.   Numbers 6:24-26 (ESV)

9.   Acts 20:32 (GNT)

Thank you for joining me on this journey to God Place. I pray this book has touched your heart in some unique way. If you genuinely enjoyed *The God Place*, would you please write a short review about it on Amazon? Here is the link directly to the page.

http://www.amazon.com/review/create-review?&asin=1733481508

Your help by sharing comments about this book is most appreciated. Reviews from readers like you make a huge difference in helping others discover the heart of God. Thanks again, and God bless you abundantly!

ACKNOWLEDGEMENTS

First and foremost, I am indebted to, and thankful for God, my heavenly Father, and my Lord Jesus Christ. They have been the primary sources of inspiration guiding me through the process of writing and publishing my first book.

There are thousands of men and women who have positively influenced my life. Their hearts are intertwined within the pages of this book.

A very special thanks to my loving wife of more than four decades. She has tirelessly given her love, support, talents and encouragement. Kim, you are awesome! Thanks to my three daughters who have also been encouraging in many ways. They have put up with my long-winded dialogues about this book and patiently endured, listening to a dream that seemed unachievable ... "Daddy, are we there yet?"

Thanks to the board of directors of The God Place, Inc. for allowing me to take on this project. Your support and insights has been empowering. Renee Schafer Horton, an author and writing teacher, taught me how to think while writing. Thanks for the introductory sessions. Adam Colwell of Adam Colwell's WriteWorks, LLC picked up the coaching baton and helped organize the initial draft of the book. This was perhaps the most involved part of writing the book. I have great appreciation for you. You are a true inspirer.

Much heart-felt thanks to the initial team who read and commented on the first draft. This includes Steve Carter, Jan Magiera, Trish Barbera, Raymond and Anamika Thomas, Diana Edeline, Donna Clayton, Bruce Williams, and Amelia Schmid. Your input was valuable in shaping the impactful message of the book. Jan Magiera continued helping with further edits and support making the manuscript even more palatable. She did this in the midst of writing her newly released book, *Sequence of Events of the End Times.* You are all amazing!

Ray Hollenbach, a published author, added further refinement to the book. He gently but skillfully edited and polished the final draft, chapter by chapter. I found Ray to be like the butcher, the baker and candlestick maker. He trimmed the excessive fat, put the icing on the cake and illuminated certain points by suggesting pull quotes to make the book a wonderful presentation. I am grateful for you!

Once the manuscript was finished, I met acclaimed author J. M. Hayes through the Writer In Residence program at our local library. Mr. Hayes kindly explained the options of the next phase of the publishing process. He referred me to Glenn McCreedy, an experienced marketing and publishing consultant who has been instrumental in navigating the various decisions of publishing and marketing concerns.

Without all of these dedicated ladies and gentlemen, the book might not have come into fruition. Thank you! Thank you! Thank you! All of you are blessed by God!

REFERENCES

WANT MORE INFORMATION?

Visit our website: www.thegodplace.org

email: sayhello@thegodplace.org